STORIES FROM THE
BALLOT BOX

Stories From the Ballot Box

HISTORY AND REFLECTIONS FROM JEFFERSON COUNTY

H.S. Leigh Koonce

To Susannah,

Thanks for supporting my book &
for your friendship.

Best,

Ellerslie Books

Many thanks to Jennifer Everhart King,
my cousin, for all of her technical and
graphic design assistance and Four Seasons
Books for acting as the premier distributor
of this book.

Contents

Foreword

By: Natalie E. Tennant,
29th West Virginia Secretary of State

It has been said voting is the right by which we have all other rights. It's a powerful and inspirational statement and makes us proud to be Americans and West Virginians.

Just as our nation has evolved in our democratic journey, so is the case with voting in America. The struggle to gain voting rights for all our citizens is well documented.

Our forefathers only granted the right to vote to white males who were landowners when the Constitution was ratified in 1787. Since then, it took the work of suffragettes to get the right of women to vote and civil rights activists to force states to remove the poll taxes and Jim Crow laws that discouraged and denied African Americans and poor whites their right to vote.

Historic legislation such as the Voting Rights Act of 1965, National Voter Registration Act of 1993 and the Help America Vote Act of 2002 have helped remove arbitrary barriers at the polls to protect our right to vote. However, the political battles continue to restrict access to the ballot box forcing Congress to debate another landmark voting rights legislation bill in 2021, For the People Act.

We often hear the phrase, "the will of the people" but how is that "will" demonstrated? At the ballot box. Our voices are heard, and our representative democracy is strengthened by ensuring all eligible Americans have access to and exercise their right to vote. Election complacency makes us weak, silences those who don't participate and allows our elected officials to only listen to a minority of voters.

Leigh's book *Stories From the Ballot Box* is an impactful narrative underscoring the importance of voting. He weaves history - both personal, regionally, and statewide - into an informative read that will benefit future West Virginia election enthusiasts and historians.

By sharing the inside story and showing the results of many local and statewide races he demonstrates the importance and power of voting. This book is a must have as part of your library for current and future reference.

Natalie E. Tennant served as West Virginia's Secretary of State from 2009 until 2017. She is the first, and so far only, Democratic woman to serve on the Board of Public Works.

Secretary of State
Natalie E. Tennant

Introduction

As I write the introduction to a book I've been toiling away on for most of my adult life, I'm struck by how much has changed in a short amount of time in Jefferson County politics. When I first became aware of the different elective offices and the various incumbents there were names like Sheriff Ed Boober, Assessor Ginger Bordier, County Clerk John Ott, Circuit Clerk Patsy Noland, Prosecuting Attorney Mike Thompson, and Magistrates Gail Boober, Mary Paul Rissler, and Bill Senseney. As of December of 2020, only Patsy is still in office, as all others have retired. Patsy, too, will be retiring at the end of the year. But then change must happen and several qualified individuals have gone on to serve in many of those positions.

A good friend of mine, Marguerite Rockwell, once remarked that she sees politics as my "sibling" because it has been such an integral part of my life. I can't say I disagree with her. Ever since I was about 13, I have been an avid watcher of elections and reader of political history. Even before then I don't remember a time when I didn't hear discussions of politics and elections at home. My parents frequently took me into the voting booth with them when I was a child. I still remember going with my Mom to C.W. Shipley Elementary School and listening to her tell me who she was "punching" on the ballot and why. When I studied political science at Shepherd, I always gravitated toward domestic political history, especially the history of women and ethnic and religious minority candidates in federal level elections.

I suppose politics is in my blood. I say this by way of explanation, not out of any sense of arrogance or boastfulness. I am privileged to be the great-great-grandson of Jefferson County's first member of the

West Virginia House of Delegates, George Koonce, who also later served as a West Virginia State Senator and as a deputy federal marshal. Another great-great-grandfather, John Allstadt, was involved in perhaps the largest political statement ever made in Jefferson County when he was kidnapped, along with his son, by John Brown and held captive in what is now known as John Brown's Fort. I also have a great-great uncle, George Johnson, who represented West Virginia's Fourth Congressional District in the United States House from 1923-1925 and again from 1933-1943. Johnson preceded one of my political heroes, Ken Hechler in holding that seat. (Maybe there is something about the name George that is lucky in politics!)

Recent generations of both sides of my family have been much more locally focused. My mother, Mary Everhart Koonce, father, Stafford H. Koonce, and paternal grandfather, Howard S. Koonce, all made bids for the Harpers Ferry County Commission seat. Unfortunately, all came up short in the Democratic Primaries. (My great-uncle, Sam Henkle, did make the cut though.) My great-aunt, Mrs. Darrell Koonce (as she liked to be known) was an associate chairwoman of the Jefferson County Republican Party and was in leadership with the State Republican Party. My uncle, William S. Everhart, was one of the last Justices of the Peace in Jefferson County. I'm a third-generation member of the Jefferson County Democratic Executive Committee, which has been the privilege of my life. My maternal grandfather, Herbert W. Everhart represented the Middleway District, my mother represented the Harpers Ferry District, and I now represent the Middleway District and serve as chairman. I believe I take after my grandfather and mother in the respect that my place, just as they saw theirs', is in the party structure at the local level, toiling away to do whatever I can do to help elect Democrats in Jefferson County.

Perhaps the most successful politician in my family is a cousin, the late Sarah Ada Koonce of Prince George's County, Maryland. She was not only the first woman elected to the Maryland House of Delegates from Prince George's County, but also served on the Prince George's County

Council and as Clerk of the County's Circuit Court. Unfortunately, she died in 2012, at the age of 90.

Thinking about the service of those members of my family and the many other elected officials, candidates, and dedicated party workers over the years has often encouraged me to work on this publication, especially when I thought of tossing it in a drawer. Being involved, even in the limited ways I have, with politics has enabled me to meet so many wonderful, caring, and interesting folks over the years. Many of those same people impressed upon me the importance of civic involvement and public service. I will be remiss to not mention, in some substance, five people who have truly aided, nourished, and supported my love of politics.

Reva Nicodemus Mickey, the grande damme of Democratic politics in Jefferson County, served eight years as chairwoman of the Jefferson County Democratic Party, the first and only woman to hold that position. A trailblazer for women in local politics, Reva hosted a baby shower for my mother when she was pregnant, with me, and I can never remember a time when I didn't know who she was. Reva has always had time to speak with me, whether it is just to share news or to offer advice on countless instances. While she has retired from active duty with the Democratic Party, she is my most trusted advisor and the first person to whom I run when I want an opinion.

John E. Ott, the longtime County Clerk of Jefferson County, is truly an institution in the Court House, though I first came to know him from very frequent visits to the lunch counter at Stuck and Alger Pharmacy, first with my parents (usually my Mom) and then on my own when I could drive. John was the type of elected official who was always in his office (except for lunch breaks) and kept a watchful eye over all of his deputies and assistants, many of whom worked decades for him. I remember fondly our discussions about local politics and while we didn't always agree we could disagree civilly, and I'm honored to call him a friend.

Al Hooper, who served a term as County Commissioner from the Charles Town District, is another person I'm privileged to know and call a friend. A few years after my Mom ran for County Commission, I made a point of attending as many meetings of the body as I could to continue my interest in local government. I came to know Al from those meetings, and the occasional lunchtime discussion at the aforementioned Stuck and Alger lunch counter! While Al and I are members of opposing political parties, he has never held that against me! During his time on the Commission, I think he played one of the most important roles in any political arena, that of consensus builder—a role that is sorely lacking in our politics today.

John D. Rockefeller, IV, former WV Delegate, Secretary of State, Governor, United States Senator, and true West Virginian, made a huge impact on me, though he wouldn't know me if I fell down in front of him. I was thrilled to serve as a summer intern in his Washington, DC office a few years before he retired. While my interactions with him were very limited, his personality could be felt throughout the office, one of kindness, concern for all people, and hard work. I will never forget the day he took those of us working as interns to lunch in the Senate Dining Room. The entire way from his office he stopped any passing fellow Senator and introduced each of us to him or her (Sens. Thad Cochran, Jeff Bingaman, Chuck Grassley, Lisa Murkowski, and Byron Dorgan). I'll always remember my time there and the mentality he insisted upon in his office that everyone do their best to help West Virginia and its citizens.

And finally, Mary Everhart Koonce. It may seem rather canned to attribute to one's parent a sense of purpose, but I passionately believe the reason I am involved in civic and political organizations today is owing to the example set by my Mother, who I so dearly miss every day. When I was growing up, I assumed everyone's parents went to one or two meetings a week for things I knew were time consuming but didn't quite understand. (Things like Garden Club, the Democrats, the Cancer Council, the PTA, the School Improvement Council, etc.) It wasn't until I became an adult that I truly realized how busy she stayed and how much she worked to improve our community, often in understated or unstated ways.

These individuals and so many more have fed my desire to work civically and politically, and I think of them often while I do it.

A Few Notes

You will find, as you read this book, that I reference information in many places, but in many others I do not. Having been active in politics for nearly two decades, I have a bundle of information rolling around in my head as to who served in what office and when. For that information I offer no citations. Further, all election returns were copied down by me from the record books in the Jefferson County Court House or the West Virginia Secretary of State's Office and are public records.

I try to include biographical data as much as possible and while it may seem piecemeal, I typically include it when a person is first mentioned. I include as much information as possible that I think readers will find interesting, but, in some cases, there are people who I either know much better than others, or more information about them is available. Additionally, I, at times, use newspaper accounts for a different year than that which I am covering, simply to offer more biographical information, in a few instances.

Senator George Koonce

Delegate Sarah Ada Koonce

Representative George Johnson

From left: Mary Everhart-Koonce, Lisa Franzen, West
Virginia First Lady Sharon Percy Rockefeller, Emma Watson,
Delegate Bianca James

Herbert W. Everhart

1

Setting the Stage

Before diving into any of the elections or facts and figures, I wish to set the stage a bit, both in the context of which positions voters decide upon, but also about the partisan control of the county. While this may be a bit boring, I think it helps readers who don't live and breathe politics to know a bit more about the various offices, the length of their terms, and the like.

Also, I start my discussion of elections with the year 2002, because that is when I truly began to pay attention to local politics.

First, though, I want to offer the below cheat sheet about when offices appear on the ballot and then I will discuss, briefly, their duties. I should point out that "off-year" elections are those that occur when the office of President of the United States is not on the ballot. Typically, those are quieter years in West Virginia and do not witness the sheer number of offices to be filled that a presidential year election sees.

I will also point out that West Virginia has a Primary Election in May. This election is when the two major parties select their candidates to face off in November and when non-partisan races (like the Board of Education) are decided. In West Virginia voters who are registered as an Independent may ask for one of the partisan ballots. Thus, if Joe is an independent voter, he can ask for a Democratic ballot or a Republican ballot, or simply choose to vote for only the non-partisan offices. He can't vote for some Democrats and some Republicans. In the General Election in November, all candidates are on the same ballot and every voter receives the same ballot. Third party candidates and Independents appear on the ballot, too.

West Virginians vote on three federal level offices. Every four years we select a presidential candidate who receives West Virginia's electoral votes (now five). The number of electoral votes is determined by the number of United States Senators (every state has two), added to the number of United States House of Representatives members (we currently have three). Our United States Senators serve six-year terms, and they are staggered, thus we don't vote on both seats during the same election year. Rather, in a six-year period there will be two different cycles with one of those seats on the ballot. Senator Joe Manchin, III is our senior Senator (first elected in 2010) and Senator Shelley Moore Capito is our junior Senator (first elected in 2014). Every two years we elect a United States House of Representatives member (sometimes called a Congressperson). West Virginia has three House Districts and Jefferson County is located in the Second District, represented by Alex X. Mooney since 2014. The entire state votes for President and United States Senate, but only the counties that fall within the Second Congressional District vote for our Representative, which explains why vote totals are always lower for this office than others.

There are currently 11 statewide elected positions in West Virginia, excluding our United States Senators. All West Virginians vote for each of these offices. They are Governor, Secretary of State, Attorney General, Auditor, Treasurer, Commissioner of Agriculture, and five Supreme Court Justices. With the exception of the Supreme Court, the other positions are collectively called the Board of Public Works. All Board of Public Works positions are four-year terms and appear on the ballot in the presidential election years. Our Board of Public Works is presently made up of:

Governor Jim Justice, first elected in 2016
Secretary of State Mac Warner, first elected in 2016
Attorney General Patrick Morrisey, first elected in 2012
Auditor J.B. McCuskey, first elected in 2016
Treasurer John Perdue, first elected in 1996
Comm. of Agriculture Kent Leonhardt, first elected in 2016

Only the Governor is term limited and may serve only two consecutive, four-year terms. Of course, a former Governor can opt to run again for a non-consecutive term. Justice was elected as a Democrat but changed his registration to Republican in 2017. Perdue is a Democrat, while the others are all Republicans.

The Supreme Court Justices serve 12-year terms and until 2016 were elected on a partisan ballot, thus they ran as a Democrat, Republican, Independent, or third-party candidate. Beginning with the 2016 election, they are now non-partisan and are chosen in the Primary Election. The terms are staggered, so unless a term is unexpired, they don't all appear at the same time on ballots. Due to the length of the terms, though, it isn't uncommon for unexpired terms to appear given illness, resignation, or even, sadly, death.

West Virginia has two state legislative bodies, the West Virginia House of Delegates and the West Virginia State Senate. The House has 100 members, and the Senate has 34 members. Delegates serve two-year terms and Senators serve four-year terms. Each Senate District (there are 17) has two Senators. Oddly, there are only 67 House Districts, but some Districts have multiple members—we haven't had a District like this in the Panhandle since 1992. So, every Delegate seat is on the ballot every two years, however the terms of Senators are staggered, so only one appears on voters' ballots each cycle. Because the lines drawn for these districts aren't county specific (meaning most delegate and senate districts cover multiple or only part of a county), it can be confusing for residents to know who they can and cannot vote for. Jefferson County has three Delegate Districts contained within the County at present. Our Senate District covers all of the county, but also includes a portion of Berkeley County, mainly centered around Martinsburg. Just like with Congressional Districts, these Districts are redrawn every ten years after the census occurs. So, the current Districts are not the ones we will have in 2022. Also, if a Senate District comprises more than one county, both Senators cannot be from the same county. Our current legislative team is:

State Senator John Unger, first elected in 1998
State Senator Patricia Rucker, first elected in 2016
State Delegate Sammi Brown, 65th District, first elected in 2018
State Delegate Paul Espionsa, 66th District, first elected in 2012
State Delegate John Doyle, 67th District, first elected in 2018

In West Virginia there are two groups of Judges who sit in Circuits, just another name for a district. Circuit Court Judges handle criminal and civil litigation, while Family Court Judges handle family law cases, divorce, child custody, etc. Depending upon the size of a Circuit, some only have one or two judges, others, like ours, have six. The 23rd Judicial Circuit covers Jefferson, Berkeley, and Morgan Counties. The 24th Family Court Circuit covers Jefferson and Berkeley Counties. Both types of Judges serve eight-year terms and are voted upon by all voters in their Circuit. Just like with Supreme Court Justices, until 2016 Judges ran under a political party. Now they are all elected on a non-partisan basis in the May Primary Election. Additionally, they run in Divisions. Oddly these divisions have nothing to do with geography, but simply delineate who runs against who. In fact, there is no geographic requirement other than that they live within the Circuit. At present five of the six Circuit Judges live in Berkeley County, with one in Jefferson, and none in Morgan. Our current Judges are:

> Circuit Judge Bridget Cohee, first elected in 2016
> Circuit Judge David Hammer, first elected in 2018
> Circuit Judge Debra McLaughlin, appointed in 2019
> Circuit Judge Steve Redding, first appointed in 2018
> Circuit Judge Michael D. Lorensen, first appointed in 2012
> Circuit Judge Laura V. Faircloth, first elected in 2016
> Family Court Judge Sally Gavin Jackson,
> > first appointed in 2001
> Family Court Judge David Greenburg, first elected in 2008
> Family Court Judge David Camilletti, first appointed in 2015.

The remainder of the offices are voted on at the county level. All counties in West Virginia have each of the following: Sheriff, Assessor, Prosecuting Attorney, Surveyor, Clerk of the Circuit Court (aka Circuit Clerk), and Clerk of the County Court/Commission (aka County Clerk), as well as five Board of Education members. All counties also have County Commissioners (or County Council members) and Magistrates, but the number varies. All of these offices are four-year terms, with the exception of the two Clerks and the five County Commissioners, who serve six-year terms. Only the office of Sheriff has term limits, with two consecutive terms being the limit. However, just like Governor, an individual can sit out a cycle after two terms and then run again. The four-year positions coincide with the Presidential elections.

A quick note, the position of Surveyor is one that comes without pay and without set duties and is usually vacant.

Jefferson County has one County Commissioner for each magisterial district (Charles Town, Harpers Ferry, Kabletown, Middleway, and Shepherdstown). The Commissioner who represents a certain district must live within that district. All county voters vote for that office, though. Many times, I encounter folks who believe the only voters who can vote for Commissioners are those who live within that district. Again, this isn't the case. Commission seats are staggered for their election cycles. For instance, in 2020, Harpers Ferry and Kabletown were up. 2022 will be Charles Town and Shepherdstown and 2024 will be Middleway.

Board of Education (aka School Board) members serve four-year terms and are staggered. Three seats are always up in off-year cycles and two in Presidential years. They are non-partisan positions, and the races are decided in the May Primary only. There is a residency requirement for this office, too, however all county residents vote for these positions. Not more than two members can be seated from any one magisterial district. For instance, if Jane, Tom, and Sue all run for the Board of Education, three seats are open, and they are the top vote getters but all live in the Middleway District, only the top two will be seated. The third seat goes to the next highest vote getter in a district other than Middleway. This can get a little confusing and while it is supposed to offer equal representation for the various districts, there are often times when certain districts will be left out. Harpers Ferry and Middleway currently have no representatives on the Board.

The position of Magistrate is the newest office in Jefferson County. In 1976 the role was created, and the positions of Justice of the Peace and Constable were eliminated. Jefferson County started out with two Magistrates and eventually a third was added. They conduct criminal arraignments, handle small claims cases, as well as some criminal matters.

Sheriff Pete Dougherty, first appointed in 2013

Assessor Angie Banks, first elected in 2008

Prosecuting Attorney Matt Harvey, first elected in 2016

Surveyor, currently vacant

Circuit Clerk Laura Storm, first appointed in 2009

County Clerk Jacki Shadle, first elected in 2016

County Commissioner Jane Tabb, first elected in 2012

County Commissioner Patsy Noland, first elected in 2008

County Commissioner Josh Compton, first elected in 2016

County Commissioner Caleb Hudson, first elected in 2016

County Commissioner Ralph Lorenzetti, first elected in 2018

Magistrate Vicki D'Angelo, first appointed in 2018

Magistrate Arthena Roper, first appointed in 2019

Magistrate Carmela Cesare, first elected in 2020

Board of Education member Gary Kable, first elected in 2006

Board of Education member Mark Osbourn,
 first elected in 2012

Board of Education member Kathy Skinner,
 first elected in 2014

Board of Education member Laurie Ogden,
 first elected in 2014

Board of Education member Donna Joy, first elected in 2020

There are a couple of other political offices in the County, those of the various Executive Committees, which are perhaps the most low-profile of any. The Democratic and Republican Parties each have a State Executive Committee, which has the same district lines as the West Virginia Senate Districts. Two men and two women are elected from each Senate District for each of the Party Committees. At the next level each county has a Republican Executive Committee and a Democratic Executive Committee. One man and one woman from each magisterial District are elected for these seats. These terms are four-years and appear on the Primary ballot in off-year elections. The chairperson of each of the Committees is the official leader of the party in that jurisdiction.

There are also two other Executive Committees that each party elects, but their only powers are to meet to appoint a replacement on the ballot if a candidate withdraws or dies. These committees are the State Senate Executive Committee and the Congressional District Executive Committee.

2

Presidential Politics

While I'd never wish to leave West Virginia, I sometimes envy those who live in New Hampshire, which is ground zero for presidential politics. For the purposes of the time period covered in this book, West Virginia has never been a swing state at the General level and our Primary is so late, the de facto nominee is typically known. Thus, we rarely get visits from Presidential candidates, with a few exceptions I will discuss in a moment.

Since 1932 there have been 22 Presidential Elections. West Virginia sided with the Electoral College winner 16 times. In 14 of those cases the Democrat was the victor, even in years that were considered large scale wins for the Republican Party. Prior to 2000, a Democratic victory was typically a foregone conclusion. Since 2000, I don't think the Republican nominee has worried much with West Virginia and has won it by a comfortable margin.

In Franklin Roosevelt's four General Election victories he carried West Virginia with 54% in 1932, 61% in 1936, 57% in 1940, and 55% in 1944. Truman, too, had little trouble winning our state in 1948, as he pulled in 57% of the vote. Even as popular General Dwight D.

Eisenhower won the Presidency in 1952, West Virginia gave its support to Democrat Adlai Stevenson, II, 52% to 48%. In 1956 this flipped, though, with incumbent Eisenhower winning the state with 54%. I wish to skip over 1960 for a moment. 1964 was a blowout year for Democratic incumbent Lyndon B. Johnson and he received 68% to Arizona Senator Barry Goldwater's 32%. Richard Nixon won a narrow victory across the country, but Vice-President Hubert Humphrey tallied 49% of the vote to Nixon's 41% and Alabama Governor George Wallace's 10%. Richard Nixon did win overwhelmingly in 1972, as South Dakota Senator George McGovern lost 49 states. Jimmy Carter was the pick of West Virginia voters in both 1976 (58%) and 1980 (49.8%). Ronald Reagan did win in 1984 with 55% of the vote, but similar to 1972, it was a nationwide sweep for the Republican. We reverted to our old ways in 1988 with Massachusetts Governor Mike Dukakis pulling in 52%, while losing across the country. Bill Clinton carried West Virginia both times, winning 48% in 1992 (Bush had 35% and Ross Perot 16%) and 51% in 1996. Clinton's victory would mark the end of the assured Democratic victory in West Virginia.

George W. Bush's 2000 win was a surprise. He received 52% of the vote to Al Gore's 46%. I don't remember much about the race, as I was too young to really appreciate what was happening, but I recall both of my parents were surprised that Gore lost. I do know John Kerry's campaign made a modest play at West Virginia in 2004, hoping his record as a military veteran would be helpful. While he tallied more raw votes, his margin of the vote was worse than Gore's. Bush won 56% in West Virginia in 2004 while Kerry received 43%. In 2008 Senator Barack Obama received 43% of the vote over Arizona Senator John McCain, but from there the tallies for Democrats have steadily decreased. Obama won only 35% in 2012 and Hillary Clinton received 26.5% in 2016, the worst showing for a Democratic candidate and, in fact, any major party candidate in the history of the state. In 2020, former Vice-President Joe Biden only improved slightly upon Clinton's performance, netting about 30% of the vote.

1960 was an interesting year for West Virginia, though, and one in which our Presidential Primary may have helped catapult John F. Kennedy to the White House. Prior to 1972, Presidential Primaries weren't nearly as powerful as they are now, and it wasn't uncommon for major contenders to totally ignore them. In 1960 a number of candidates sought the presidency, including Massachusetts Senator John F. Kennedy, Minnesota Senator Hubert H. Humphrey, and a number of favorite-son candidates—see more about this below. There was a thought at the time that a Catholic candidate couldn't win in an overwhelmingly Protestant state, which West Virginia was and is currently. In 1960 a televised debate between Kennedy and Humphrey took place in Charleston. It was the first of the 1960 season and thought to be only the second televised Primary debate up until that time.[1] A number of books have recently been released about John Kennedy and his 1960 White House run and those interested should definitely take a look.

Both Senators Kennedy and Humphrey made campaign stops in Jefferson County that year.[2] John Kennedy visited the Charles Town Race Track on April 27th. *The Spirit of Jefferson* reported over 3,000 attendees and billed it as "the biggest political rally ever staged in the county." The paper added, the same day, that Reverend Robert E. Lee Strider, the retired Episcopal Bishop of West Virginia and a resident of Leetown, endorsed Kennedy.[3] Bishop Strider's niece, Carrie, was the first female sheriff in Jefferson County and readers will learn more about her in Chapter 3.

2008 also bore witness to a Presidential candidate visit. Then-Senator Hillary Rodham Clinton made a campaign stop in Shepherdstown on May 7th, 2008, as she and fellow Senator Barack Obama remained in the race for the Democratic nomination. Clinton was accompanied by her daughter Chelsea Clinton and was introduced by Shepherd University President Suzanne Shipley and endorsed by WV

Delegate Bob Tabb. Clinton went on to win the race in WV with 67% of the vote to 26% for Obama and 7 % for former North Carolina Senator John Edwards.

I do want to touch upon the concept of a favorite son presidential candidate, mainly because our own Senator Robert C. Byrd was one in 1976. The concept of a favorite son candidacy has largely died out, but it was very prevalent up until the last part of the 20th century. A candidate would place himself on the ballot in only his home state, likely win that state, and then be able to go to the convention with a set of delegates and presumably release them at his will to a candidate of his choosing, and possibly have enough delegates to yield some clout in matters before the convention. So, even though there were over a dozen Democratic candidates running for the nomination in 1976, only Senator Robert Byrd and Alabama Governor George Wallace appeared on the ballot in West Virginia. Byrd, of course, won very handily, totaling 331,639 votes to Wallace's 40,938. Byrd didn't appear on any other state ballots, so the only delegates he received going to the convention were those of West Virginia.

There was some talk of Senator Jay Rockefeller running, not as a favorite son, but as a full-fledged candidate in 1992. There are even campaign buttons, but while he may have considered it, he never entered the race. Rockefeller's uncle, Nelson Rockefeller, had run as a Republican several times and served as President Ford's Vice-President. Another uncle, Arkansas Governor Winthrop Rockefeller, ran as a favorite son in his home state in 1968. Nelson Rockefeller also ran that year, and as best I can tell, it's the only time two brothers received delegate votes at a major party convention in the same year.

Only one major party presidential nominee has ever come from West Virginia, John William Davis, who was nominated by the Democratic Party in 1924, but who lost to Calvin Coolidge. His father, John J. Davis, attended the second Wheeling Convention, along with my great-great-grandfather, to deal with the question of succession and later served in the United States House in the 1870s. Oddly enough, Cyrus Vance, who was President Jimmy Carter's Secretary of State was Davis's adopted son. Vance's son, Cy, is now District Attorney for New York County. Politics is certainly a small world.

Davis's road to the Democratic nomination was exceedingly long. He wasn't officially the Democratic candidate until 103 convention ballots had been cast! He and his running mate, Charles Bryan, faced not only the Coolidge/Dawes ticket but also the Robert LaFollette and Burton Wheeler ticket, which was nominated by the Progressive Party, the Farmer-Labor Party, and some affiliates of the Socialist Party. It ended up as a blowout election for the Republicans. Coolidge took 54% of the vote and 35 states, good for 382 electoral votes. LaFollette won his home state of Wisconsin and 4,831,706 votes, approximately 17% of the vote. Davis received 29% of the vote, 8,386,242, and just 12 states. He lost West Virginia and every state outside of the South, winning Texas, Oklahoma, Arkansas, Louisiana, Mississippi, Alabama, Tennessee, Virginia, North Carolina, South Carolina, Georgia, and Florida.

Davis was born in Clarksburg, West Virginia on April 13, 1873. He served one term in the United States House of Representatives from 1911 until 1913 and was then appointed United States Solicitor General in Woodrow Wilson's Cabinet, a position he held until 1918. After that he was United States Ambassador to the United Kingdom through 1920 and was briefly a candidate for President that year. He died in Charleston, South Carolina in 1955.[4]

I will be remiss to not mention Jefferson County's own presidential candidate, Angus Wheeler McDonald, who ran in 1988 (3,604 votes), 1992 (9,900 votes), and 2000 (19,374 votes). McDonald's campaigns released a couple of buttons, and he ran newspaper ads, including in the local *Spirit of Jefferson*. McDonald still resides in Jefferson County on his farm outside of Charles Town.

While our state may not realize my dream of being a major battleground for presidential candidates, our neighbors to the north (Ohio and Pennsylvania) and our neighbor to the east (Virginia) get to have some of the fun.

[1] Phil Kabler, "Historic 1960 Humphrey-Kennedy Debate Took Place in WV," *Charleston Gazette-Mail* (Charleston, WV), Jul. 27, 2015.

[2] "Battleground West Virginia: Electing the President in 1960," West Virginia A&H, West Virginia Division Archives and History, Dec. 26, 2019, http://www.wvculture.org/history/1960presidential campaign/counties/jefferson.html.

[3] "Kennedy Given Rousing Welcome by Over 3,000 Democrats at Biggest Political Rally Ever Staged in County," *The Spirit of Jefferson* (Charles Town, WV), Apr. 28, 1960.

[4] William DeGregorio, *The Complete Book of U.S. Presidents* (Fort Lake, NJ: Barricade Books, 2009), 200.

Ambassador John W. Davis
The Library of Congress

3

Women in Jefferson County and West Virginia Politics

I start this chapter as I will many others, with some personal reflections. From an early age I can remember both of my parents, but especially my mother, discussing local politics. It never occurred to me that political offices are often viewed as gendered, until I really dug into historic election results. At no point do I have a recollection of ever hearing at home, "That candidate can't win because she's a woman." For that I am thankful.

State Legislative Elections

While the overall representation of women in politics in West Virginia doesn't top the list, we do hold a very important distinction. On January 10th, 1928, Minnie Buckingham Harper became the first African American woman to be seated in a state legislature in the country.[1] Additionally, she was only the sixth woman to serve in the West Virginia House of Delegates.[2] No women had served in the

West Virginia State Senate at this point. Harper arrived in the House as many women did during the first half of the 20th century, by appointment owing to the death of her husband.

Born in Winfield, West Virginia (Putnam County) on May 15, 1886, Harper married E. Howard Harper and moved to McDowell County where she was a homemaker. Upon the death of her husband, she was unanimously recommended by the McDowell County Republican Executive Committee to be appointed to complete his term and Governor Howard Gore made it official. Delegate Harper opted not to seek election to a term in her own right, yet her place in history was secure. She later remarried and died in Winfield on February 10th, 1978.[3]

I regret that even those of us who are quite plugged into West Virginia politics and political history don't know much about Delegate Harper. Natalie Tennant, our former Secretary of State, has mentioned Harper, along with former Secretary of State Helen Holt and other prominent women in West Virginia politics when talking about our state's rich history.

While this book specializes in Jefferson County politics, I do want to continue to digress and touch upon women in state politics a bit more. The 1920s saw the first seven women seated in the WV House, four by election and three by appointment. The first was Mrs. Tom (Anna) Gates, a Democrat from Kanawha County, who was elected in 1922 for one term. 1924 saw two women win seats, Mrs. Thomas J. Davis, a Republican from Fayette County, and Dr. Harriet B. Jones, a Republican from Marshall County. Delegates Davis and Jones only served a single term each. Two women were appointed in 1926, Jefferson County's own Hannah Cooke (more on her in a minute) and Mrs. Fannie Anshutz Hall, a Democrat from Wetzel County. Again, neither delegate returned after the completion of her appointed term.

From this point on, the number of women in the West Virginia State Legislature gradually ticked up.[4]

The year 1934 saw the first woman to hold the office of West Virginia State Senator, Mrs. Hazel E. Hyre, a Democrat from Jackson County. She was appointed on March 12th to complete the term of her husband. Five years later Mrs. John C. Dice, of Greenbrier County, was appointed as a Democrat to serve out the rest of the late William Jasper's term. While Jefferson County was on the forefront of the service of women in the WV House, it wasn't until 1965 that a woman represented a district including Jefferson in the WV Senate. On January 11th Governor Hulett Smith appointed the widow of Senator Donald J. Baker to complete his term. Senator Betty H. Baker was elected in her own right in 1966. The Bakers were based in Hardy County, which was then part of the same district as Jefferson.[5]

In a few pages I will take a closer look at the women who have served Jefferson County in the State Legislature; however, I wish to first discuss women making bids for statewide office. For those interested in reading more about the women who have served in the West Virginia Legislature, the source I cited has a wonderful timeline.

Statewide Elections

While I've so far focused on state legislative service, there is much to be said about women holding statewide and local office as well. To situate us on the national stage, the first woman to be elected to a statewide office was Laura Eisenhuth of North Dakota. She was elected as a Democrat to the position of Superintendent of Public Instruction in 1892.[6] Ninety-six years later, West Virginia elected its first woman to statewide office, Supreme Court Justice Margaret Workman.[7] While she was the first woman elected to statewide office, she wasn't the first to serve. In 1957 Helen Holt was appointed

West Virginia Secretary of State, a position she held until her defeat in the 1958 General Election.[8]

The first woman to be nominated for statewide office was Mrs. Donald Clark of Wayne County. She ran as the Democratic nominee for Secretary of State in 1924. Here is an excerpt from *The Wayne County News*:

"She is prominently known throughout the State, having long been active in social, political, and religious work of various organizations. During the war Mrs. Clark led Red Cross activities in her home county. She served on the State Child Welfare Commission. Until recently she was president of the board of education in her home district and was instrumental in a number of important improvements among the schools in her charge."[9]

Clark, a Democrat, had been recruited to run for Congress from the Fifth District against Wells Goodykoontz, who won by special election in 1919, but she declined. According to the article, her father, Samuel Sperry Vinson, was one of the "strongest political characters of Southern West Virginia." Further, the article offered glowing reviews of a speech she had recently given at a Democratic meeting in Parkersburg.[10]

When the votes were tallied, Clark came up short by about 33,000 votes out of approximately 575,000, receiving 260,206 votes to 293, 254 for Republican George W. Sharp and 7,491 for Socialist W.F. Naylor. Clark did win Jefferson County with 4,432 votes to 1,866 for Sharp and 34 for Naylor. While she didn't win, Clark made history as the first woman to run statewide as a major party nominee for office.

It didn't take long for another woman to run for Secretary of State. In 1928 Mrs. William Campbell was the Democratic nominee to face incumbent Secretary Sharp. Campbell was from Jefferson County and the only woman to run for statewide office in the state's history to come from our county, although we did have a US Senate nominee later on. Unfortunately, I've been unable to locate much information about her other than a few newspaper articles and the official election returns. According to *The Spirit of Jefferson*, she was elected as the associate chairwoman of the Jefferson County Democratic Executive Committee in 1928.[11] *The Farmers Advocate* gave front page coverage to a campaign appearance she made in Rippon on October 24th.[12] Campbell didn't win or come as close as the Democratic nominee did in 1924. She pulled in 279,516 votes, while George Sharp received 352,084 votes. Campbell did win Jefferson County, but she lost Berkeley and Morgan by fairly large margins.

It wasn't until 1957 that a woman was seated as a statewide officeholder. Helen F. Holt was offered the position of Secretary of State by then-Governor Cecil Underwood, and she accepted. The position was vacant owing to the death of incumbent D. Pitt O'Brien that year. Holt's deceased husband, Rush D. Holt had served as a Democrat in the United States Senate, having been elected at the age of 29, but later became a Republican and unsuccessfully sought the office of governor in 1952. Originally from Illinois, at the time of her appointment Holt was on the faculty of Greenbrier College. Her graduate degree was in zoology, and she had served on the faculty at other colleges prior to working at Greenbrier.[13]

Once she was sworn in, Holt announced she planned to run for the office when her term was up in 1958. No stranger to campaigning, she had worked with her husband during his many campaigns, including for the United States House in 1950, Governor in 1952, and WV House in 1954. Rush Holt was serving in the WV House at the time of his death and Governor William Marland appointed Helen Holt to serve the rest of the term, which ended in 1957. She opted not to seek election in her own right.

I write about a visit Secretary Holt made to Jefferson County in a later chapter. I have to say it was a pleasure to meet her and have a brief conversation. She died in 2015, just a few weeks shy of her 102nd birthday. Her son, Rush Holt, Jr., was a member of Congress from New Jersey for many years and visited the Panhandle for at least one Democratic Party event.

After Secretary Holt left office, it was 30 years before another woman would hold statewide office. Kanawha County Circuit Court Judge Margaret "Peggy" Workman won a seat on the WV Supreme Court of Appeals, thus becoming the first female Justice and the first woman to win a statewide race. Elected as a Democrat, Workman came in second in the Democratic Primary, edging out incumbent Justice Darrell McGraw by about 6,000 votes. The other incumbent, Justice Thomas Miller was also re-nominated. In the November General, Workman and Miller were easily elected over Republicans Charlotte Lane and Jeniver Jones. Supreme Court terms are for 12-years, so Workman was assured a seat on the court until 2000.

Workman resigned in 1999, shortly before her term expired. In 2002, she entered the Democratic Primary for the Second Congressional District's seat in the United States House of Representatives. Also running was the 2000 nominee, Jim Humphreys, who lost a close race to Shelley Moore Capito that year. Workman came up short against Humphreys, receiving 29,888 votes to Humphreys 31,597. She won Jefferson County by about 350 votes. Humphreys would go on to lose to Capito in a rematch. Had Workman been the nominee, it would have been the first time two women faced off for a seat in the US House from West Virginia in the state's history. She also would have been only the third woman to have served in Congress from West Virginia and the only one who didn't have a family member who had also served.

Workman ran again for the Supreme Court in 2008. Two seats were on the ballot that year, those held by Justice Elliott "Spike" Maynard and Justice Larry Starcher. Maynard filed to run again, while Starcher announced he planned to retire. Two other Democrats joined Workman and Maynard on the ballot, Huntington attorney Menis Ketchum and WVU Law Professor Bob Bastress, the husband of WV Delegate Barbara Evans Fleischauer. Beth Walker was the only Republican to run. Workman came in first with 35.97% of the vote, followed by Ketchum who received 27%. Maynard was defeated, receiving 19.4% of the vote. In Jefferson County, Workman was again first with 41.56% of the vote, followed by Bastress with 21.67%, Ketchum at 21.18%, and Maynard was last receiving 15.59%.

The General Election was surprisingly close, as most Democratic candidates skated to election in statewide races that year. Ketchum came in first with 355,778 votes, Workman was second with 336,346 votes, and Walker was very close behind with 329,395. Justice Workman and Ketchum joined incumbent Justices Robin Jean Davis, Brent Benjamin, and Joseph Albright. The make-up of the Court remained four Democrats and one Republican and returned to its all-time high of two women serving. In 2020, Workman announced she would not run for re-election, thus completing her second, non-consecutive 12-year term and becoming the longest serving female WV Supreme Court Justice.

Margaret Lee "Peggy" Workman was born in Charleston on May 22, 1947. Her father was a coalminer, and the family has deep roots in Boone County. After receiving an undergraduate degree from WVU, she graduated from the College of Law in 1974 and entered private practice. In 1981 Governor Rockefeller appointed her to an open judgeship in Kanawha County. She was elected to the remainder of the term in 1982 and won a full term in 1984. Workman resigned from the Circuit Court in 1989 to take her seat on the Supreme Court. She served terms as Chief Justice in 1993, 1997, 2011, 2015, and

2018.[14] In 2020 she was given the West Virginia Democratic Party's highest honor, the Robert C. Byrd Award, for her decades of service as an elected Democrat.

I met Justice Workman for the first time when she ran for Congress, and we were always a Workman household when she appeared on the ballot.

The second woman to be elected to the Supreme Court was Robin Jean Davis, who was elected to an unexpired term in 1996. Franklin Cleckley, the only African American Supreme Court Justice in the state's history, chose not to run for election, after having been appointed by Governor Caperton in 1994. Vying for the rest of the term, along with Davis, were Danny Staggers of Keyser and Circuit Judge Booker T. Stephens of Welch. Staggers is the son of the late Congressman Harley O. Staggers, Sr. Davis won the Democratic nomination with 45% of the vote, with Staggers at 34.7%, and Stephens receiving 20.3% of the vote. In the general election she prevailed with 318,955 votes to Republican David M. Pancake's 217,772 votes.

Her election made her only the second woman to win statewide and marked the first time that more than one woman sat on the Supreme Court. Since this was an unexpired term, Justice Davis would face votes again in 2000.

Four Democrats filed for two seats on the Court in 2000. Incumbent Justice Robin Jean Davis sought a full term. She was joined by former Supreme Court Justice Joe Albright, State Senator and future Justice Evan Jenkins, and WVU Law Professor Bob Bastress. Albright served by appointment between September 26th, 1995, and December 31st, 1996. Voters picked Albright (131,948 votes) and Davis (108,230 votes) to be the nominees for the General Election, a result mirrored in Jefferson County. The lone Republican who filed was former State Senator and Kansas Judge John C. Yoder of Harpers Ferry.

In the General Election Justices Davis and Albright were both elected to their first full, 12-year terms on the WV Supreme Court of Appeals. Albright garnered 366,833 votes, Davis took 309,804 votes and Yoder finished with 218,195. Justice Albright replaced appointed Republican Justice George M. Scott of Roane County, reverting the Court back to 5 Democrats, as Albright joined Davis and Justices Warren R. McGraw, Spike Maynard, and Larry Starcher. Davis was now the lone woman, with the 1999 resignation of Justice Margaret Workman.

Justice Davis opted to seek another term in 2012 and was joined by five other Democrats. Justice Albright had died in office in 2009, and former Justice Thomas McHugh was appointed and then elected in 2010 to the remainder of the term. McHugh decided to retire, so there would be one open seat in the 2012 cycle as well. Aside from Davis, attorneys Letitia "Tish" Chafin, H. John Rogers, and Louis Palmer, as well as Circuit Judges Jim Rowe and J.D. Beane all filed for the two seats. The results weren't particularly close, with Davis at 27.9% and Chafin at 27%. They were followed by Rowe at 19.8%, Beane at 10.3%, Rogers at 9.2%, and Palmer at 5.8%. Two Republicans ran, John Yoder and Allen Loughry.

Justice Davis was successful in her quest for a second term, receiving 294,882 votes, the most of the four candidates. The second highest vote getter was Republican Allen Loughry, who took 284,299. Yoder finished third with 258,213 votes and Chafin was last with 248,284 votes. Had Chafin been successful, the Court would have been majority female for the first time in the state's history.

Robin Jean Davis was born in Van, Boone County on April 6th, 1956. Her parents worked as a coal miner and a teacher. After receiving an undergraduate degree from West Virginia Wesleyan College, she earned graduate and law degrees from West Virginia

University. She engaged in private practice until her election to the Court in 1996. Justice Davis served as Chief Justice in 1998, 2002, 2006, 2007, 2010, and 2014. She resigned on August 14th, 2018, following the approval of impeachment proceedings approved by the State House regarding expenses relating to remodeling the Supreme Court offices.[15]

The third woman to serve on the WV Supreme Court is Beth Walker, who had run previously, including against Justice Workman in 2008. When Republicans took over control of the state legislature in 2015, they passed legislation to make all judicial races non-partisan, with voters making their selection during the Primary Election only. Incumbent Justice Brent Benjamin, who had been elected as a Republican in 2004 filed to retain his seat. Also running were former Justice and Attorney General Darrell V. McGraw, Jr., former legislator Bill Wooton, and former prosecutor Wayne King. Walker won with a plurality of the vote, taking 162,245 votes. McGraw received 94,538, Wooton 84,641, Benjamin 51,064, and King 17,054 votes. With Walker's election the Court now had three women and two men, marking the first majority female period in the Court's history.

With the resignation of Justice Davis and the retirement of Justice Workman, the court will have only one female member for the foreseeable future.

Aside from Justice of the Supreme Court, Secretary of State has been the only other office to which women have been elected on a statewide basis, with the exception of Senator Shelley Moore Capito. In 2004 Republican Betty Ireland became Secretary of State and served for one term. The office was then won by Democrat Natalie Tennant, who held it until 2016. The only other woman to have served on the Board of Public Works is Lisa Hopkins, who was appointed to fill out the remaining months of Glen B. Gainer, III's final term as West Virginia State Auditor. Hopkins did not seek the office. I will cover these office holders in future chapters.

Women in Federal Elections

Before a deep dive into Jefferson County politics, I'd be remiss not to mention Congressional races. Again, to situate ourselves I'll note the first woman to be elected to the United States House of Representatives was Jeannette Rankin, a Democrat from Montana. She served a single term from 1917-1919 and then another term from 1941-1943.[16]

While it took West Virginia a while to match Montana, it wasn't for want of trying. In 1922 Izetta Jewell Brown ran for the United States Senate from West Virginia. Her late husband, William G. Brown, Jr., had been a member of the United States House. Brown, a former actress, was the first woman to run for the United States Senate on a major party ticket from a state south of the Mason-Dixon Line. She lost the Democratic Primary to M.M. Neely by only 6,000 votes. She ran again in 1924 for the other Senate seat, but lost another close primary, this time to William E. Chilton. She remarried in 1925 and moved to New York, where she made an unsuccessful bid for a seat in the US House in 1930. Brown also made headlines as the first woman to second a presidential nomination for a major party candidate. In 1920 she made the seconding speech for John W. Davis and again in 1924, when he successfully captured the Democratic nomination.[17]

In 1951, Maude Elizabeth Kee was elected in a special election to fill out the remainder of her husband John Kee's term representing the Fifth Congressional District (mainly counties in the southern party of the state). Kee was then elected to seven terms in her own right, before retiring and being succeeded by her son, James.

Born in Radford, Virginia on June 7, 1895, Maude Simpkins was the seventh of 11 children. Her parents were conservative, Republican Baptists, and as soon as she was old enough Kee converted to Catholicism and registered as a Democrat. She worked as a secretary for *The Roanoke Times* and later as a court reporter. Her first marriage, to James Frazier, ended in divorce and she later married the attorney (John Kee) who represented her ex-husband. Elizabeth Kee served as the executive secretary to her husband when he entered the US House in 1933. While working for her husband, Kee described her role as "being all things to all constituents" and summed it up as being a "clergyman, lawyer, psychiatrist, and family friend."[18]

John Kee died on May 8th, 1951, during a committee meeting. Within a week of his death Elizabeth Kee announced her intention to seek the remaining year and a half of his term. She was apparently not the favored candidate of the Democratic establishment at the time and was offered a position as secretary to whomever won. Unsurprisingly the overture greatly irritated her. Her son, and eventual successor, James heavily lobbied the United Mine Workers for their support; the tactic worked, and she won. Kee was sworn into office on July 26th, 1951 and became the first woman to serve in Congress from West Virginia. She was also the first woman in the state to serve in elective office at a level above the state legislature.[19]

In total Kee served a little more than 14 years and was considered a fairly liberal Democrat. She focused heavily on veterans' affairs and chaired the Subcommittee on Veterans' Hospitals. Her district was one of the top producing coal districts in the country, which, understandably, made issues facing miners and the coal industry of top concern to her. In 1964 she announced she wouldn't seek another term, owing to declining health. James Kee won the seat and served continuously until the seat was eliminated in redistricting in 1972. The Kees were the first husband-wife-son combination to serve in Congress and she was the first member to be succeeded immediately by her son.[20]

Only two other women have represented our state in the US House, Shelley Moore Capito, a Republican, who held the Second Congressional District seat from 2001 until 2015, and Republican Carol Miller who was elected in the Third Congressional District in 2018. Only one woman has been elected to the United States Senate, Capito, who began her first term in 2015.

Born in 1953 in Glen Dale, WV, Shelley Moore obtained undergraduate and graduate degrees from Duke University and the University of Virginia, respectively. She worked as a counselor at West Virginia State University and later as the director of the education information center for the West Virginia Board of Regents.[21] Capito served from 1997-2001 in the WV House from Kanawha County, a seat her son, Moore Capito, now holds. When Bob Wise declined to run for re-election to the US House in 2000, in order to run for Governor, Capito filed and beat attorney Jim Humphreys by two points to become the first Republican member of Congress since 1983, the first Republican woman to represent WV in Congress, and only the second woman period. She continued to be re-elected every two years until 2014 when she ran for and was elected to the United States Senate, defeating Secretary of State Natalie Tennant. Not only is the Capito the first and only woman to represent WV in the Senate, but she also became the first Republican in the upper chamber from our state since 1959. She was re-elected by approximately 40 percentage points in 2020, against Democrat Paula Jean Swearengin.

Her father, Arch A. Moore, Jr., served a term in the WV House, six terms in the US House, and three terms as Governor. He was defeated once for US House, once for US Senate, and twice for Governor. In 1990, Governor Moore was found guilty of mail fraud and spent two years in federal prison. From the best I can tell Moore,

Capito, and Moore Capito are the only father, daughter, grandson combination to have served in the WV Legislature.[22]

The only other woman to represent WV in the Congress is Carol Miller, who was elected in 2018 and 2020. Born in 1950 in Columbus, Ohio to Congressman Samuel L. Devine and Betty Devine, Miller was first elected to the WV House in 2006, defeating incumbent Democrat Margarette Leach. She continued to be elected every two years and became the first female majority whip in the WV House.[23] In 2018, with incumbent Evan Jenkins filing to face US Senator Joe Manchin, the WV-03 seat was open. Miller filed, along with former Delegate (and former Democrat) Rupie Phillips, Dr. Ayne Amjad, and Conrad Lucas, the chairman of the WV Republican Party. Miller came in first with 23.8% of the vote, followed by Phillips with 19.5%. She faced State Senator and veteran Richard Ojeda in the general. What was thought to be a competitive race turned out not to be so. Miller won 56% of the vote to Ojeda's 43.6%. She entered the US House as the only freshman Republican woman that year.

In 2020, all four Democratic nominees for the US Congress, Paula Jean Swearengin (US Senate), Natalie Cline (WV-01), Cathy Kunkel (WV-02), and Hilary Turner (WV-03) were women, again a first in the state's history.

I wish to mention two notes of interest relating to women in federal office from WV. First, of the three woman who have served, all have had a familial connection to the US House. Elizabeth Kee's husband served immediately prior to her. Capito's father and Miller's father both served in the House as well, although not directly before them. Miller's father also represented the state of Ohio, rather than West Virginia. The next point of interest is that in both of Capito's US Senate races she faced a female Democrat. From what I can tell, though I may be in error, she is the only female United States Senator to face a female opponent in two consecutive races.

Another National First

In 1920 Leena Lowe Yost became the first woman in the United States to preside over a Republican state party convention. Born in 1878 in Marion County, Yost graduated from West Virginia Wesleyan College. She served for a decade as president of the Women's Christian Temperance Union's West Virginia Chapter and as president of the West Virginia Equal Suffrage Association. Additionally, Yost spent four years as head of the Women's Division of the national Republican Party. She was the first woman to serve on the West Virginia State Board of Education. Living into her 90s, she died in 1972 in Washington, DC.[24]

Jefferson County Women in the WV Legislature

I wish us to straddle the line between local and state politics for a moment and discuss the women who have been elected by Jefferson County to serve in the West Virginia Senate and the West Virginia House of Delegates.

As I mentioned a few pages ago, the first woman to represent Jefferson County in the WV House was Hannah Cooke. Born on October 27, 1878, at Duffields, Hannah Washington Alexander was a well-known figure in the County. She and her husband, Delegate E.E. Cooke owned and operated Washington, Alexander, and Cooke Insurance and Surety Bonds. When he died the Jefferson County Democratic Executive Committee unanimously recommended her for the vacancy on January 3rd, 1926. Governor Howard M. Gore then appointed her on January 27th, and she served one year before retiring and returning to work in the County.[25] Delegate Cooke holds the distinction of being the fourth woman to serve in the WV Legislature and has descendants still living in Jefferson County today.

The next woman to represent Jefferson County was Margaret Potts Williams, another Democrat, who was appointed by Governor M.M. Neeley on November 19th, 1941, to fill the unexpired term caused by the death of Delegate William Alexander. The Farmer's Advocate newspaper offered brief coverage of the process:

"The Democratic County Executive Committee, at a special meeting Friday night, with Chairman J.W. Lynch presiding, selected three possible appointees to succeed the late William F. Alexander ... Presented for the Governor's selection were Mrs. W.F. Alexander, the widow of the deceased legislator, Reynolds Moler, of Shepherdstown, who contended with Mr. Alexander for the Democratic nomination for the House of Delegates in the May Primaries; and Mrs. Margaret Potts Williams, an active Democratic worker in Shepherdstown."[26]

I remember my Mother speaking of "Mrs. Williams," but never in a political context. She was involved in a number of civic organizations, including some of the garden clubs in Jefferson County. Her family owned Popodicon, which is now the residence of the President of Shepherd University. Prior to the renovation of the grounds of the Jefferson County Court House, there was a boxwood that had been planted in her honor. It has since been removed.

The next woman to serve our area in the legislature was Betty H. Baker of Hardy County. While Jefferson County and a small piece of Berkeley County now comprise our WV Senate District, it used to be much larger, as was the case when Senator Baker was elected. Born in 1919 at Thomas, WV, Betty Head was the daughter of Harry D. and Kathryn Agnes Higgins Head. She received her Bachelor of Science degree from West Virginia University, where she served as the first female student body president. Her first husband was killed in

World War II, and she later married Donald J. Baker, who was elected to the WV Senate in 1964 with 52% of the vote.[27] Upon his death she was appointed to the vacancy on January 11, 1965 and ran for the remaining two years of his term in 1966. Senator Baker defeated John I. Rogers 13,543 votes to 11,154. She then ran for a full term in 1968, but was defeated by Rogers by approximately 145 votes, although she carried Jefferson County by a wide margin. After her defeat Senator Baker remained very active in the Moorefield, Hardy County area. She died at Grant Memorial Hospital in Petersburg, WV, on November 12, 2011, at the age of 92.[28]

After the defeat of Senator Baker, Jefferson County only had to wait two years to see another woman in the WV Senate. Republican Louise Leonard, who was the 1968 Republican nominee against WV Delegate Roger Perry, shook the political landscape when she defeated incumbent Senator Clarence E. Martin, II, by 1,200 votes in the 1970 General Election. Her victory was surprising for several reasons. First, aside from the victory of Rogers over Betty Baker the previous cycle, it wasn't the habit of the District to send Republicans to Charleston. Second, Senator Martin was regularly re-elected by wide margins (unopposed in 1954, 69%-39% in 1958, 58%-42% in 1962, and 54%-46% in 1966). Martin, also, was from a prominent family in Martinsburg and a respected local attorney. Nonetheless, Leonard defeated him and set out for Charleston in 1971.

Born in Washington, DC on October 7th, 1919, Louise McVey was the daughter of Roy Leslie McVey and Florence Alberta Bellows McVey. She attended the George Washington University School of Government and married Robert P. Leonard on January 23, 1948. Upon arriving in Harpers Ferry, Leonard became heavily involved in a wide variety of civic organizations, including serving as first vice president of the West Virginia Federation of Republican Women. She was also appointed by Richard Nixon to a four-year term on the advisory board of the Federal Reformatory for Women in Alderson, WV.[29]

In 1972 Senator Leonard decided to challenge incumbent United States Senator Jennings Randolph, who was first elected in 1958. Randolph easily defeated Leonard, polling 486,310 votes to Leonard's 245,531. I have heard repeated postulation from folks who were alive at the time, that her decision to challenge Randolph led to her defeat in 1974 while seeking a second term in the WV Senate. She received 48% of the vote to attorney Bob Steptoe's 52%. It is worth noting, however, that Leonard was the first woman to be nominated by a major party for a United States Senate seat in West Virginia and would remain the only one until 1996 when Republicans nominated Betty A. Burks to challenge Jay Rockefeller.

In 1976, two Democrats sought the nomination for the 36th District's seat in the WV House, comprising almost all of Jefferson County, the incumbent James L. Moler and Carolyn Snyder. In a close race, Snyder edged Moler with 2,295 to his 2,108. In the General she beat Thomas Kitchen 4,731 to 2,052, thus becoming the first woman to be *elected* to the WV House from Jefferson County, and the third woman from our county to serve, after appointed Delegates Hannah Cooke and Margaret Potts Williams. Snyder served until 1977 when she resigned to become the Eastern Panhandle representative for Governor Jay Rockefeller. Snyder re-entered politics in 1990 when she ran for a seat in the WV Senate. She came in second to Sondra Moore Lucht, receiving 3,974 votes to Lucht's 4,809, and 2,741 for James C. Smith. Snyder is still active in the community, as a real estate broker, and served several terms on the State Democratic Executive Committee.

Carolyn M. Snyder was born in Binghamton, New York, the daughter of Christopher J. and Elizabeth Bowman Hoagland. She obtained her undergraduate and graduate degrees and pursued doctoral work at Columbia University. Snyder taught at a number of institutions, including Queens College and Pace University and worked for IBM, among other businesses. Most recently she founded Snyder, Bailey, and Associates, a real estate firm based in the Eastern Panhandle.[30]

Replacing Snyder in the WV House was Democrat Bianca M. James, whose appointment was announced by Governor Rockefeller on October 12th, 1977. The Democratic Executive Committee submitted three names to Rockefeller. Former Delegate James Moler and James Louthan were the other two suggested. At the time of her appointment, James was the manager for the Martinsburg Laundry and Dry Cleaning Company's Charles Town office. Upon making the appointment Rockefeller said, "I am confident she can, and will, do a competent job representing the people of Jefferson County in the W.Va. legislature."[31]

James ran for the Democratic nomination for a full term in 1978, but she was defeated in a three-way primary. Moler received 1,856 votes, James 887, and 433 votes went to Agnes Thomas. In 1980 former Delegate James filed for the Charles Town seat on the County Commission. She again placed second, this time in a crop of four candidates. Robert D. Ott received the most votes with almost 1,500. James took 1,073. The incumbent Commissioner, Charles J.W. Smith came next, and then Charles Town Councilman Edward Braxton. After her loss James remained involved in Democratic politics and other organizations. She later worked at the John Brown Wax Museum in Harpers Ferry. James died in 2012, at the age of 90.[32]

Bianca Maria Visconti James was born on July 27th, 1922, in Milano, Italy. She graduated from St. Ursula Academy in Italy and studied music at the Milano Conservatory of Music Studies until World War II broke out. James married an American soldier and immigrated to the United States and became a citizen. She served four terms on the Democratic Executive Committee and several terms as president of the Democratic Women's Club.[33] I remember my Mom speaking frequently of Delegate James, but I don't recall if I ever met her. In addition to her work with politics, she is remembered for her tireless support of the Old Opera House, which has a rehearsal space named after her son, Thomas "Tommy" James.

It wasn't too long before another woman entered the Legislature from a district including Jefferson County. In 1982, Sondra Moore Lucht filed for the 16th Senate District. As I mentioned when Senators Baker and Leonard were elected from the same district, it covered much more territory than it does now. Lucht, a resident of Martinsburg, was joined by Fred Butler (Inwood), Terry T. Harden (Berkeley Springs), Daniel P. Lutz, Jr. (Charles Town), Edward Morrow (Martinsburg), and Roy Stroupe (Shepherdstown). The breakdown of votes was fairly interesting. Morrow won Berkeley County, followed by Butler and then Lucht. Morrow won Jefferson County, followed by Lucht and then Butler. Harden won Morgan County, followed by Lucht. Lucht won Hampshire, Hardy, and the small portion of Mineral that was included in the district. In the end, she tallied 3,245 votes, with Morrow winning 2,632, and Harden at 2,328. On the Republican side, County Commissioner Gary Lee Phalen was nominated without opposition. In the November general, it was a close race with Lucht receiving 16,855 votes and Phalen 15,896. A note of interest, they each won the other's home county. This makes sense, though, as Berkeley has always been more Republican than Jefferson.

Lucht ran for re-election in 1986 and faced no primary opponent. The Republican Party appointed Harry Dugan, a businessman from Berkeley County, to run in the general. Lucht prevailed, winning every county except Morgan. She received 14,500 votes and Dugan took 10,730.

As I wrote earlier in this chapter, the 1990 Democratic Primary for this race featured three candidates. Lucht was re-nominated against Carolyn Snyder and James C. Smith, all of Berkeley County. Lucht won Berkeley, Hampshire, Hardy, Jefferson, and Mineral. Snyder won Morgan County. She was re-elected in the November General without Republican opposition.

Senator Lucht filed for a fourth term in 1994. Owing to the census, the District had been redrawn and shrunk in geographic territory, now only encompassing Berkeley, Jefferson, and Morgan Counties. Terry Harden, who had run in 1982, challenged Lucht in the Democratic Primary. He won Morgan County by a small margin, though Lucht won the other two counties by at least a two to one margin. The Republican Primary was fairly crowded in 1994. Dugan filed again, as did John R. "Rick" Bartlett and David Michael Myers. Again, all candidates were from Martinsburg. Dugan won with 3,422 votes to 1, 607 for Myers, and 1,070 for Bartlett. 1994 was dubbed the Republican Revolution in Washington, DC, with sweeping victories for the party across the country. West Virginia Republicans, however, saw only modest gains, but the revolution did pass through the 16th. Lucht last to Dugan by about 1,300 votes out of almost 25,000. Her service of 12 years, though, has made her the longest serving female legislator from a district that includes Jefferson County.

Sandra Moore Lucht attended Glenville State College, Marshall University, and James Madison University and worked as a school psychologist. She has been involved in a number of civic and political organizations, including as president of the WV National Organization for Women, a member of the WV Education Association, the Board of Directors of Gateway Youth Home for Boys, and the Board of Governors of the WV Women's Hall of Fame. In 1982 she received the Susan B. Anthony Award.[34] Lucht was the last woman to serve in the WV Senate from the Eastern Panhandle until 2016, when Patricia Rucker was elected.

When Senator Lucht left office in 1994, it took 14 years before another woman represented our county in the WV Legislature. Tiffany Lawrence sought and won the 58th Delegate District seat in 2008. She served until 2014, when she lost to Republican Jill Upson, who in turn lost to Democrat Sammi Brown in 2018. I won't go into detail about these races here, as I cover them in the chapters about the years in which they took place further along in the book.

Women in Jefferson County Offices

Now that I've digressed for a couple of pages, I'll bring us back to the central focus of this chapter—women in Jefferson County politics. To simplify things, I will highlight four offices: Sheriff; County Commission; Assessor; and Magistrate and offer an extended discussion of each.

Jefferson County made national news when the appointment of Carrie Strider as the new Sheriff was announced in 1948. Many of the headlines are horribly dated to modern audiences. *The Hope Star* of Hope, Arkansas proclaimed, "Bishop's Niece Becomes Sheriff, But Without Gun."[35] *The Hagerstown Herald* offered "Young Woman Is Sheriff: Jefferson County Brunette Hopes There Will Be No Wave of Crime." The article began with "Miss Carrie Lee Gardner Strider, statuesque 37-year-old brunette..." and dedicated a paragraph to her interest in knitting.[36] Thankfully Jefferson County coverage was a bit more sedate. While the *Spirit of Jefferson* did include the news on its front page, the short article spent as much time talking about the length of service of her deputies (all men) as it did covering her appointment.[37] Still, Sheriff Strider's service was an important first for Jefferson County and as of the writing of this book, no other woman has served as Sheriff.

"By action of the Jefferson County Court Monday morning, January 5th, Miss Carrie Lee Strider was appointed Sheriff of Jefferson County to fill the unexpired term of the late Garland H Moore.

Sheriff Strider's appointment runs to December 31, 1948, which office will then be filled on January 1, 1949, by results of the November election.

Miss Strider first assumed the duties of Deputy Sheriff on April 1, 1937. She was appointed by R.J. Madison who served nearly two full terms till January 1, 1945, when he was succeeded by the late Garland H. Moore.

Following her appointment Sheriff Strider announced the appointment of Charles Dodson, Herbert Rogers (Shepherdstown), and Garland H. Moore, Jr. as deputies.

Deputy Sheriff Dodson first assumed office in 1945 under Garland Moore's appointment; Herbert Rogers took office in 1939; and Garland H. Moore, Jr.'s appointment as office deputy is new.

Shortly after noon, Monday, a large bouget of flowers appeared on the new Sheriff's desk, a remembrance from some of her friends and well-wishers."[38]

The first woman to be elected to countywide office in Jefferson County was Louise P. "Tucky" Corbin. In 1960 she was one of six candidates to seek a seat on the Jefferson County Board of Education. Joining her on the ballot were Conrad "Connie" Hammann, C. DeForest Boyer, Leo J. Widmyer, W.O. McCoughtry, Jr., and Charles Printz. An interesting note to mention is that Printz, Hammann, and Corbin all lived in the Charles Town District. At that time, and still presently, only two members of the Board can live in the same Magisterial District. At the time one Board member, Shirley M. Hunt, was already serving from Charles Town. Thus, if Hammann and Corbin received the most votes, the second-place finisher would not be seated.[39]

On Election Day, Louise Corbin finished first with 2,614 votes, thus becoming the first woman to be elected to a countywide position in Jefferson. Widmyer, of the Harpers Ferry District, came in second with 2,269 votes, and Printz was third with 2,170. There were three seats open at the time, two regular, six-year terms, and one unexpired term with less than a year remaining, owing to the resignation of John Rissler.[40] Even though Printz lived in the Charles Town District, he seems to have been seated anyway and I can't find an explanation for this action, as it seems to mean that three Board members lived in the Charles Town District. Regardless, Corbin served out her six-year term as the first woman on the Jefferson County Board of Education.

More can certainly be written about female candidates for the Board of Education and perhaps I shall in a future volume.

Jefferson County's governing body, the County Commission, is an excellent example of the snail's pace at which women have been elected in West Virginia. It wasn't until 2001 that a woman was seated on this five-member body, but not for want of trying. From what I can tell, the first woman to be nominated by either political party for County Commission was Dorothy W. Conklyn, who was nominated by the Republican Party in 1970 for the Charles Town County Commission seat. It was an unexpired term lasting only two years. In 1972 the Republican Party nominated Jane Duffy for the Harpers Ferry seat. Neither Conklyn nor Duffy won the General Elections which they contested. Six years later Reva Mickey came a close second in the Democratic Primary for the Kabletown County Commission seat.

It wasn't until 1992 when another woman was nominated by either party; the Democratic nomination for the Shepherdstown seat went to Dorothy McGhee. On the eve of the 21st century, Jefferson County was, after 137 years, going to witness a woman on the County Commission.

The year 2000 saw the first time two women were nominated by their respective parties for a seat on the County Commission. The retirement of two-term Commissioner Edgar Ridgeway left an open seat from the Middleway District. The Republican nomination went to Jane Tabb. The Democrats lined up behind Delores Milstead after a five-way Primary. Tabb moved to Jefferson County when she married Lyle C. "Cam" Tabb, III, whose family has been engaged in farming for generations. Her late father-in-law was also a longtime chairman of the Jefferson County Democratic Party and her brother-in-law, Robert C. "Bob" Tabb was elected to the West Virginia House of Delegates in 2002. Milstead, too, moved to Jefferson County and settled in Middleway, where she and her family purchased an historic home. Both candidates were active in a variety of county civic organizations. In the end, voters kept the all Republican membership of the Commission intact by electing Tabb.

Commissioner Tabb remained the lone woman on the Commission for her entire first term. In 2006 she was defeated in a close race by Democrat Frances Morgan, an attorney, who also has a family background in farming. With Morgan's victory, the balance shifted to three Democrats (she joined 2004 victors Dale Manuel, of Charles Town, and Jim Surkamp, of Shepherdstown). The dam broke in 2008 with the election of two Democratic women to replace two Republican men. Former Magistrate and long-time Circuit Clerk Patricia A. "Patsy" Noland was elected from the Kabletown District, replacing A.M.S. "Rusty" Morgan, III. Noland was first elected as a Magistrate in 1984 and served until 1994, when she was elected, in a special election, to the position of Circuit Clerk. The Harpers Ferry seat was won by Lyn Widmyer, a long-time community activist and planner, who lives at Federal Hill Farm. With the victories of Widmyer and Noland, the County Commission was completely in Democratic hands for the first time since 1978. The momentum, however, slowed here.

2012 brought familiar territory. Tabb filed to run for her old seat and dispatched a primary challenger. She defeated Morgan, which meant the number of women on the County Commission remained at three but was now two Democrats and one Republican. In 2014 the Democratic Party re-nominated Patsy Noland for the Kabletown seat and Ronda Lehman for the Harpers Ferry seat, as Widmyer announced her retirement. Lehman is no stranger to civic organizations in Jefferson County and has a professional background in nursing and medical legal work. Noland was unopposed in the General, but Lehman was defeated by Republican newcomer Eric Bell (who later resigned from the Commission under a legal and ethics cloud). The balance of power was now back in Republican hands and the number of female commissioners dwindled to two.

In 2016 Democrats nominated Jan Hafer, who grew up in Middleway and Shepherdstown, for the Shepherdstown seat. She had returned to Jefferson County a few years prior after retiring as a professor from Gallaudet University. A well-known community figure, she was Executive Director of the Shepherdstown Visitor's Center at the time of her filing. In what turned out to be a bad year locally for Democrats, she came up short to Caleb Hudson, who had defeated incumbent Walt Pellish in the Republican Primary.

In 2018, Commissioner Tabb chose to run for the fourth time, and it appeared it would be the fourth cycle for that seat in which two women squared off. Tabb drew a primary opponent. Democrats had no candidate until the last day of filing when Carol Grant threw her hat in the ring. Grant retired as the top civilian at the United States Coast Guard and was active in numerous civic organizations in Jefferson County, including a short term as president of the Organization of

Democratic Women. However, after the primary election Grant withdrew her candidacy. The Democratic Party appointed attorney and farmer Robert Barrat, who faced Tabb in the General. In another close election, Tabb prevailed.

As the 2020 Election approached, Commissioner Noland declined to seek a third term. Retired Army Lt. Colonel Lanae Johnson was unopposed in the Democratic Primary and faced Republican Steve Stolipher in the General Election. Also up was incumbent Ralph Lorenzetti of the Harpers Ferry District. Two Republicans filed to face him, Gary Cogle and Tricia Jackson. Jackson ended up winning the Primary and defeated Lorenzetti in a surprising upset. Johnson, too, was defeated in another bad year for Democrats. As 2021 begins, the Commission will still have two women members, but will be all Republican for the first time since 2004.

While it may seem I'm painting a dim picture of the history of women in County Commission races, I am happy to say the 21st Century brought us, kicking and screaming, into some degree of equity.

The position of Jefferson County Assessor is one that seems to attract long term holders, which is, I believe, for the best as on-the-job training isn't ideal for the intricacies of the work. I can reflect upon this office more personally than most, as my Mom was employed in the office at different points under three different incumbents. While her employment there was largely before I was born, I have fond memories of going with my Mom to the office to visit longtime Assessor Ginger Bordier and other staff. Not only was Ginger the Assessor from 1981 until 2009, but she had worked in the office prior, retiring after 55 years with the Jefferson County government. A notorious smoker, I think Ginger probably smoked at her desk until the day she retired. A number of employees who are with the Assessor's office at present were hired by Ginger and she regularly had employees who retired with decades of service in her office. One of the more entertaining stories

I recall from my Mom entailed the two of them going to see a horror movie together that no one in the office wanted to see—I believe it was *The Exorcist*. Ginger also volunteered quite heavily for the Democratic Party over the years, serving as Treasurer for the Democratic Association and as a regular ticket salesperson. Certainly, Ginger was one of a kind.

The first woman to hold the position of Assessor was Kathryn L. Trussell, who was elected by special election in 1962 and served until 1981 when Bordier took over. She and her sister Marie, who worked in the Circuit Clerk's office for three decades and lived to be 100, lived in Charles Town. As a child I recall their names often being mentioned in the house, though as with most people when I was younger, I don't, unfortunately, have as many personal memories as I'm sure others do. Kathryn and Marie always sent us cards at the holidays, and I remember receiving graduation money from Marie when I graduated from Goretti.

When Bordier announced her retirement in 2008, four people jumped into the Democratic Primary, including former Jefferson County Sheriff Ed Boober, former Jefferson County Surveyor John Kusner, and Angela L. "Angie" Banks, who had worked in the Assessor's office for several years. It was the first contested primary for the office since 1960. Banks received 39% of the vote, followed closely by Boober who polled 35%. They were followed by Kusner with 15% and Jerri Herbert at 11%. Banks also won the November General against Gary Dungan, a retired banker and active member of the county and state Republican Parties. Banks was re-elected in 2012, 2016, and 2020. The position of Assessor has been occupied by a woman longer than any other elected position in Jefferson County, some 67 years.

The position of Jefferson County Magistrate is a fairly new one in the grand scheme of things. The office first appeared on the ballot in 1976 as a partisan office. Prior, each magisterial district had Justice of the Peace and Constable elected positions. In 2016 all judicial offices in West Virginia became non-partisan and divided by division, rather than a top vote getter system. I decided to focus on the Magistrate positions, because for a fair period of time all the seats were held by women. There has also been little change in the occupants of the seats until recently.

In 1984 two women were elected and one man, a third seat having been recently added. E.W. Day, an inaugural Magistrate and a former Justice of the Peace was re-elected for his final term. Joining him were Patricia Noland and Gail C. Viands (now Boober), who had been an assistant to a previous Magistrate, Pete Dougherty. Noland and Boober were both re-elected in 1988 and 1992, when they were joined by Katherine Santucci. As previously mentioned, Noland became Jefferson County Circuit Clerk in 1994 and a special election was held to fill her seat. Both nominees were women, the Democrat Mary Paul Rissler and the Republican Jeri Willingham. Rissler prevailed and she, Boober, and Santucci were all re-elected in 1996, resulting in an all-female Magistrate team for nearly a decade.

2000 brought a change when term-limited Sheriff Bill Senseney jumped into the race, along with Stacey McDonald. In the Primary, Boober, Rissler, and Senseney prevailed and were all successfully re-elected in 2004, 2008, 2012, and 2016. Senseney retired in 2018 after over 25 years of elected service and was replaced by his assistant Vicki D'Angelo. Rissler, too, retired in 2019 after 25 years as a Magistrate and Board of Education member Arthena Roper was appointed to the vacancy, becoming the first African American Jefferson County Magistrate and judicial official. Both D'Angelo and Roper announced their intentions to retain their offices in 2020, while Boober declared she will retire after nearly 40 years on the bench. Voters retained D'Angelo and Roper and chose attorney Carmela Cesare to take over from Boober.

There is much that can be written about women in other political offices in Jefferson County, including as County Clerk, Circuit Clerk, and the Board of Education and perhaps I shall in another book. The only offices in which no women have served are Surveyor and Prosecuting Attorney.

[1] I.D. Talbott and Charles M. Murphy, "Minnie Buckingham Harper," The West Virginia Encyclopedia, West Virginia Humanities Council, May 15, 2018, http://www.wvencyclopedia.org/articles/259.

[2] *Chronology of Women in the West Virginia Legislature 1922-2009.* Charleston: West Virginia Legislature's Office of Reference & Information, 2009.

[3] I.D. Talbott and Charles M. Murphy, "Minnie Buckingham Harper," The West Virginia Encyclopedia, West Virginia Humanities Council, May 15, 2018, http://www.wvencyclopedia.org/articles/259.

[4] *Chronology of Women in the West Virginia Legislature 1922-2009.* Charleston: West Virginia Legislature's Office of Reference & Information, 2009.

[5] *Chronology of Women in the West Virginia Legislature 1922-2009.* Charleston: West Virginia Legislature's Office of Reference & Information, 2009.

[6] "Milestones for Women in American Politics," Center for American Women and Politics, Rutgers Eagleton Institute of Politics, Dec. 26, 2020, http://www.cawp.rutgers.edu/facts/milestones-for-women.

[7] Kay Michael, "Margaret Workman," The West Virginia Encyclopedia, West Virginia Humanities Council, May 7, 2019, http://www.wvencyclopedia.org/articles/1347.

[8] "Mrs. Holt Takes Secretary Post; Resigns College Office," *Charleston Gazette* (Charleston, WV), Dec. 5, 1957.

[9] "Mrs. Donald Clark, of This County, Announces for Secretary of State," *Wayne County News* (Wayne, WV), Jan. 17, 1924.

[10] Ibid.

[11] "News of Other Years," *Spirit of Jefferson* (Charles Town, WV), Jun. 24, 1948.

[12] "Mrs. Campbell at Rippon," *Farmers Advocate* (Charles Town, WV), Oct. 20, 1928.

[13] "Mrs. Holt Chosen W.Va. Secretary: Ex-Solon's Widow in Interim Position," *Charleston Daily Mail* (Charleston, WV), Dec. 4, 1957.

[14] Kay Michael, "Margaret Workman," The West Virginia Encyclopedia, West Virginia Humanities Council, May 7, 2019, http://www.wvencyclopedia.org/articles/1347.

[15] "Robin Jean Davis," West Virginia Encyclopedia, West Virginia Humanities Council, Aug. 14, 2018, http://www.wvencyclopedia.org/articles/2314.

[16] *Women in Congress 1917-2006* (Washington: United States House of Representatives Committee on Administration, 2006), 37.

[17] Jerry Bruce Thomas, "Izetta Jewell Brown," West Virginia Encyclopedia, West Virginia Humanities Council, Sep. 27, 2012, http://www.wvencyclopedia.org/articles/667.

[18] *Women in Congress 1917-2006* (Washington: United States House of Representatives Committee on Administration, 2006), 293-6.

[19] *Women in Congress 1917-2006* (Washington: United States House of Representatives Committee on Administration, 2006), 293-6.

[20] *Women in Congress 1917-2006* (Washington: United States House of Representatives Committee on Administration, 2006), 293-6.

[21] *Women in Congress 1917-2006* (Washington: United States House of Representatives Committee on Administration, 2006), 800.

[22] "Arch Alfred Moore, Jr.," West Virginia A&H, West Virginia Division Archives and History, Dec. 24, 2019, http://www.wvculture.org/government/governors/arcmore.html.

[23] "U.S. House 3 Candidate: Carol Miller," *Herald-Dispatch* (Huntington, WV), Sep. 20, 2018.

[24] Barbara J. Howe, "Leena Lowe Yost," West Virginia Encyclopedia, West Virginia Humanities Council, Dec. 9, 2015, http://www.wvencyclopedia.org/articles/1393.

[25] *West Virginia Blue Book*. (Charleston: West Virginia Legislature, 1926).

[26] "Mrs. Williams to Fill Term of Late W.F. Alexander," *Farmers Advocate* (Charles Town, WV), Nov. 21, 1941.

[27] Obituary of Betty H. Baker, *Cumberland Times News* (Cumberland, MD), Nov. 13, 2011.

[28] Ibid.

[29] *West Virginia Blue Book*. (Charleston: West Virginia Legislature, 1971).

[30] *West Virginia Blue Book*. (Charleston: West Virginia Legislature, 1977).

[31] "Bianca James is Named to House Delegate Post," *Spirit of Jefferson* (Charles Town, WV), Oct. 13, 1977.

[32] Obituary of Bianca Maria Visconti James, *Spirit of Jefferson* (Charles Town, WV), Dec. 19, 2012.

[33] Ibid.

[34] *West Virginia Blue Book*. (Charleston: West Virginia Legislature, 1987).

[35] "Bishop's Niece Becomes Sheriff, But Without Gun," *Hope Star* (Hope, AR), Feb. 19, 1948.

[36] "Young Woman is Sheriff: Jefferson County Brunette Hopes There Will Be No Wave of Crime," *Morning Herald* (Hagerstown, MD), Jan. 06, 1948.

[37] "Miss Carrie Lee Strider Named Sheriff of County," *Spirit of Jefferson* (Charles Town, WV) Jan. 7, 1948.

[38] "Miss Carrie Lee Strider Named Sheriff of County," *Spirit of Jefferson* (Charles Town, WV) Jan. 7, 1948.

[39] "May be Hard To Determine Winners for School Board," *Spirit of Jefferson* (Charles Town, WV) May 5 1960.

[40] "Selected By Voters As New Members Jefferson County Board of Education" *Spirit of Jefferson* (Charles Town, WV) May 12, 1960.

Delegate Minnie Buckingham Harpers
WV Blue Book

Delegate Anna Gates
WV Blue Book

Former Secretary of State Helen Holt (seated, center)
campaigning for Natalie Tennant in 2014.

Justice Margaret Workman
WV Blue Book

Judge Robin Jean Davis
WV Blue Book

Justice Beth Walker
WV Blue Book

Izetta Jewell Brown
The Library of Congress

Representative Maude Elizabeth Kee
The Library of Congress

Senator Shelley Moore Capito
The United States Senate

Representative Carol Miller
The United States House of Representatives

Delegate Hannah Washington Alexander Cooke
WV Blue Book

Senator Betty H. Baker
WV Blue Book

Senator Louise Leonard
WV Blue Book

Delegate Carolyn Snyder
WV Blue Book

Delegate Bianca M. James
The Spirit of Jefferson

Senator Sondra Moore Lucht
WV Blue Book

Delegate Tiffany Lawrence
Shepherd University Archives

Delegate Jill Upson
WV Blue Book

Senator Patricia Rucker
WV Blue Book

Delegate Sammi Brown
WV Blue Book

Sheriff Carrie Strider
The Jefferson County Museum

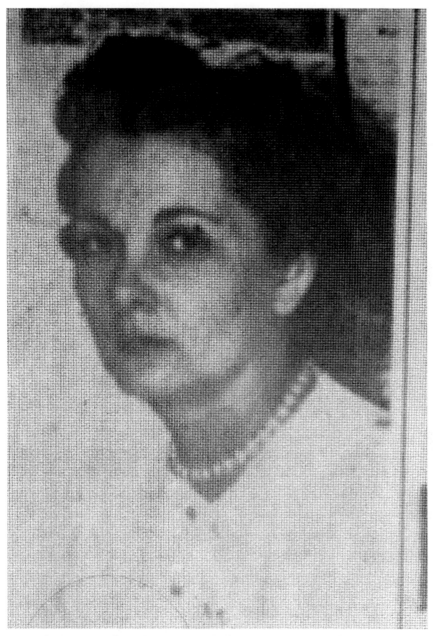

Jefferson County Board of Education Member Louise "Tucky" Corbin
The Spirit of Jefferson

4

African Americans in Jefferson County Elections

I wish to write about some highlights relating to the representation of African Americans in local and state elections, too. Unfortunately, Jefferson County, and West Virginia as a whole, have not seen the equity many other areas have in diversification of elected officials.

In Jefferson County, three African American men and one African American woman have served on the Board of Education. Dr. Madison Briscoe was appointed to an unexpired term on the Board of Education in 1975 and served until the end of 1976.[1] Also serving were Q.D. Fleming (1978 until 1984), C. Larry Togans (1994 until 2002 and again from 2013 until 2014), and Arthena Sewell Roper (2018 until 2019).

I found an article from *The Hagerstown Morning Herald* which covered Dr. Briscoe's appointment to the Board of Education. There was a vacancy on the Board owing to the death of Bill Hammond in January of 1975. Over 50 people applied for the vacancy. Briscoe, a retired professor, at first received two votes, those of Carolyn Hoffman and Conrad C. Hammann. Board member Kenneth Sims nominated William J. Brown, who had been the next highest vote getter in the previous election. After voting for Brown, Sims changed his vote so that Briscoe's appointment would be unanimous of those in attendance.[2]

According to the newspaper Hoffman expressed that one of her reasons for supporting Briscoe was that "in view of the fact that it is extremely difficult getting a black man elected (in this county) to the school board."[3] It is regrettable that the paper led with that information and not his background and involvement in the community. Briscoe resided in Harpers Ferry and received his PhD from Catholic University, after having concluded undergraduate studies at Lincoln University and Columbia University. A medical researcher, specializing in medical parasitology and entomology, Briscoe taught at Dillard University, Storer College, and Howard University. Originally from Winchester, he was 71 at the time of his appointment, which was to last until the 1976 election.[4] Briscoe is also the subject of the 2017 film *Briscoe: Man of Substance and Science.*

Briscoe did file to retain his seat, along with 14 other people. Three seats were before voters, a full six-year term, held by C.C. "Connie" Hammann, and two partial terms. The partial terms were held by Briscoe and Martha Josephs, who had been appointed to the vacancy of Carolyn Hoffman, who resigned when she moved out of Jefferson County. I won't list all the candidates, but the top vote getters were G. Warren "Jim" Mickey (2,732 votes), Paul R. Manzuk (2,160 votes), Phillip T. Porterfield, III (1,907 votes), Josephs (1,850 votes), William J. Brown (1,785 votes), Hammann (1,655 votes), Pam Parziale (1,500 votes), and Briscoe (1,239 votes). Mickey received the full six-year term, while Manzuk and Porterfield replaced Briscoe and Josephs. With this shift the Board was now comprised only of white men.

Two African American candidates ran for the Board of Education in 1978, with one being elected to a six-year term. Larry Creamer and Q.D. Fleming both filed that year, along with Pam Parziale, Kenneth H. Sims, Elise M. Stiles, James "Dixie" Wiltshire, Howard Carper, Jr., and Robert D. Ott. Sims, the incumbent, and Fleming were victorious.

Fleming ran an ad in *The Spirit of Jefferson* directly before the election, which offered biographical information. While a native of West Virginia, Fleming spent time teaching, coaching, and serving as a principal in Georgia before returning to Jefferson County in 1947. In addition to teaching here, he, again, coached and retired from an administrative position at Jefferson High School in 1977.[5] I know he taught at Charles Town High School, at one point, as I found a photograph of him in one of the yearbooks.

Fleming served as president of the Jefferson County Parks and Recreation Commission, along with other civic work, and had been elected to the Charles Town City Council. A graduate of Tuskegee Institute in Alabama, he also studied at George Washington University, WVU, and Pennsylvania State.[6] He was unsuccessful in his quest for a second term on the Board of Education in 1984, as was his fellow member, Ken Sims. Fleming finished fifth, as voters rallied around G. Warren Mickey and Pete Dougherty.

Larry Togans was the next African American elected to countywide office in Jefferson County. In 1994 he won a four-year term on the Board of Education, as terms had been shortened from the previous six-year length. Togans was re-elected in 1998, but was defeated, with the rest of the incumbent members, in 2002. When Board member Pete Dougherty resigned in 2013, to accept an appointment as Sheriff of Jefferson County, Togans was selected to serve until the next election. He chose not to run again.

A native of Jefferson County, Togans retired, in 2001, as the deputy human resources chief for the US Geological Survey. A Navy veteran, Togans received four Bronze Stars during the Vietnam War. He has long been involved in a wide range of civic and community organizations, including the Jefferson County Schools Cultural Diversity Committee, the United Way, and the Shepherd University Foundation.[7]

In 2018, Arthena Sewell Roper, sought one of the three seats up that year. At the time she was serving as the Cultural Diversity Facilitator and Staff Development Coordinator for Jefferson County Schools. Roper finished third, knocking off incumbent A. Scott Sudduth and making her the first African American woman on the Board of Education.

Roper, a West Virginia native, earned a BA from WVU, and three Masters' Degrees, including one from WVU in Public Administration and one from Marshall University in Teaching. Prior to her time with the Jefferson County School System, she was an assistant professor with the WVU Extension Service in Berkeley County.[8]

From what I can tell Dr. Briscoe was the first African American in Jefferson County to hold countywide office. There had been African Americans who held municipal office prior, including Board of Education member Q.D Fleming and Edward Braxton, both of whom served on the Charles Town City Council. Additionally, Briscoe wasn't the first African American to seek countywide office. The Rev. Joseph E. Washington made a bid for the Board of Education in 1970. Washington was the minister of the Mt. Zion A.M.E. Church in Duffields, right across from the MARC Station. He also served as president of the Local 87 of the Industrial Union of Marine and Shipbuilding Workers of America at Badger-Powhatan Plant in Ranson during their strike of 1976.[9] In 1972, James A. Tolbert, too, sought a seat on the Board of Education. Mr. Tolbert was a vigorous and well-known community member and past president of the West Virginia NAACP. Charles Town City Council member Edward Braxton ran for the Democratic nomination for County Commission, representing the Charles Town District in 1980. He finished fourth, with the nomination going to Robert D. Ott.

As I write this, only one African American holds office in Jefferson County, Arthena Sewell Roper, who is sitting as the first African American magistrate in our county. Roper had been elected to the Board of Education in 2018 but resigned when Judge David Hammer appointed her to take over from Magistrate Mary Paul Rissler, who retired in November of 2019, after 25 years on the bench.

The number of African Americans seeking office in Jefferson County has increased in the 21st Century. In 2008, retired Charles Town Police Chief Louie Brunswick ran in the Democratic Primary for Sheriff. He finished a strong second in that race to Bobby Shirley. Brunswick was also one of three finalists for the appointment, made by the County Commission, to the position of Sheriff after Shirley's resignation in 2013.

In 2016, two African American candidates filed for the Board of Education. Erica Logan and Ronald Jones both sought a seat, as two were open. I cover their candidacies in greater detail in the chapter that corresponds to that year.

In 2020, Lanae Johnson was the Democratic nominee for the County Commission seat from Kabletown, making her the first African American nominee for that body. A retired Lt. Colonel, Johnson is active in a number of organizations around the County.

African Americans in Legislative Races

The first African American to serve in the West Virginia Legislature was Delegate Christopher Payne, who was elected in 1896 as a Republican from Fayette County. Born in Monroe County on September 7th, 1848, Payne found work first as a farm hand and then as a servant in the Confederate Army. After the Civil War, he attended night school and became a teacher in Summers County and later a Baptist minister in Hinton. A noted newspaperman, he was responsible for the establishment of three newspapers: the *West Virginia Enterprise*; *The Pioneer*; and the *Mountain Eagle*. Payne eventually was appointed to a civil service job with the IRS and pursued the study of law at the same time. President Theodore Roosevelt offered Payne the position of Consul General to the Danish West Indies in 1903. Once the islands were acquired by the United States in 1917, Payne remained and became a prosecuting attorney and then a police judge in St. Thomas. He died there on December 5th, 1925.

Three African Americans have represented Jefferson County in the House of Delegates, Terry Walker, Jill Upson and Sammi Brown. Walker was appointed to the vacant 56th District, a now defunct district that covered part of Berkeley County, as well as Leetown, Kearneysville, and Middleway, in 2009 and both Upson and Brown were elected from the 65th Delegate District, which covers Charles Town and Ranson. Walker served until 2011, Upson served from 2015 through 2019 and Brown from 2019 until 2021. As best I can tell, this is the first and only time one African American female legislator was followed by another one. I will cover all three Delegates in the Chapters discussing the years they served.[10]

African Americans in Statewide Office

Only one African American has served in statewide office, West Virginia Supreme Court Justice Franklin Cleckley. Born in Huntington on August 1st, 1940, he received a B.A. degree in 1962 from Anderson College, a J.D. from Indiana University in 1965, and a LL.M. from Harvard in 1969. During the Vietnam War he served as a JAG officer. Upon graduation from Harvard, he took a position at the West Virginia University College of Law and was granted a full professorship in 1972, the first African American to be designated as such.[11]

In 1994 Governor Gaston Caperton appointed Cleckley to a vacancy on the West Virginia Supreme Court. He served until the term expired in 1997 and didn't seek election, preferring to return to WVU to teach. He retired in 2013 and died in Morgantown on August 14th, 2017. Cleckley was the author of *The Evidence Handbook for West Virginia Lawyers* and *The West Virginia Criminal Procedure* Handbook.[12]

Since Cleckley's service, there have been two African American nominees for statewide office. In 2008 Charles Minimah was the Republican nominee for Secretary of State. Democrat Natalie Tennant was elected. In 2016 and 2020 the Democratic Party nominated Mary Ann Claytor for the position of West Virginia Auditor. In both races she came up short to J.B. McCuskey.

[1] Judith Jenner, "Briscoe Named to Jefferson Board," *Morning Herald* (Hagerstown, MD) Jan. 28, 1975.

[2] Ibid.

[3] Judith Jenner, "Briscoe Named to Jefferson Board," *Morning Herald* (Hagerstown, MD) Jan. 28, 1975.

[4] Judith Jenner, "Briscoe Named to Jefferson Board," *Morning Herald* (Hagerstown, MD) Jan. 28, 1975.

[5] *Spirit of Jefferson* (Charles Town, WV) May 4, 1978.

[6] Ibid.

[7] Christine Miller Ford, "Togans Tapped for School Board Vacancy," *Spirit of Jefferson* (Charles Town, WV) Apr. 10, 2013.

[8] "New CTMS Principal, Cultural Diversity Facilitator Are Named," *Spirit of Jefferson* (Charles Town, WV) Dec. 4, 2003.

[9] "Primary Election Ballot in County Will Not Be Long, But School Board, County Court Races to Draw Voters," *Spirit of Jefferson* (Charles Town, WV) Feb. 12, 1970.

[10] "Christopher D. Payne," West Virginia A&H, West Virginia Division Archives and History, Dec. 24, 2019, http://www.wvculture.org/history/archives/blacks/payne.html.

[11] Larry Soins, "Franklin D. Cleckley," West Virginia Encyclopedia, West Virginia Humanities Council, Mar. 22, 2021, https://www.wvencyclopedia.org/articles/1294.

[12] Larry Soins, "Franklin D. Cleckley," West Virginia Encyclopedia, West Virginia Humanities Council, Mar. 22, 2021, https://www.wvencyclopedia.org/articles/1294.

Jefferson County Board of Education Member Dr. Madison Briscoe
Storer College Archives

Jefferson County Board of Education Member Q.D. Fleming
The Spirit of Jefferson

Jefferson County Board of Education Member Larry Togans
The Spirit of Jefferson

Magistrate Arthena Sewell Roper
Renee Ferguson Photography

Retired Lt. Colonel Lanae Johnson

Justice Franklin D. Cleckley
WV Supreme Court

Delegate Terry Walker
WV Blue Book

Delegate Christopher Payne
WV Blue Book

Charles Minimah

Mary Ann Claytor

5

The Election of 2002

I've decided to start with the Elections of 2002 as those are the first that I have a real memory of for several reasons. First, my Mom, Mary Everhart Koonce, made a run for County Commission that year, which caused me to become aware and involved for obviously selfish reasons. Second, though I may sometimes feel and act as though I'm in my 80s, I'm really not that old and I can't say as a pre- and early teen that I watched county politics as much as I do now.

The highest office on the ballot in 2002 was the United States Senate seat held by Jay Rockefeller. First elected in 1984, he announced plans to run again and faced two opponents in the Democratic Primary, Bruce Barilla and Bill Galloway. Neither gained much traction and Rockefeller was easily renominated with 90% of the vote. There was a contested Republican Primary, as well, between former West Virginia State Senator M. Jay Wolfe and Hiram "Bucky" Lewis. Wolfe was nominated, besting Lewis by about 17,000 votes.

There really wasn't much doubt that Senator Rockefeller would be re-elected, but I don't think he took the race for granted. I remember seeing Rockefeller signs and swag at Democratic events. On

Election Day he easily prevailed with 63% of the vote to Wolfe's 37% and received a fourth six-year term.

Much of the interest that year was focused on the race for the Second Congressional District seat in the United States House of Representatives. State Delegate Shelley Moore Capito, the daughter of former Governor Arch Moore, was the surprise winner in 2000, defeating attorney Jim Humphreys, who had also served in the West Virginia State Senate and State House of Delegates. Capito received 48% of the vote in 2000 to Humphreys 46% and Libertarian John Brown's 6%. Humphreys opted to seek a rematch but didn't have a clear path to the nomination.

Former West Virginia Supreme Court Justice Margaret Workman, the first woman elected statewide, launched a bid to face Capito. I remember meeting both Humphreys and Workman and our household was strongly in the Workman camp. It seemed to me that selecting someone who had a proven record of winning across many counties might be the ticket to success. Humphreys barely edged past Workman, taking 51% to her 49%.

In the General Election Capito greatly improved upon her margin, defeating Humphreys by 20 points. Her victory made her the first Republican to win re-election to Congress from West Virginia since her father, some 40 years prior. While she remained the only Republican representing West Virginia, she held the distinction of being the first Republican woman ever to serve from the state.

Many of the state legislative races in 2002 played out as expected. Senator John Unger was re-elected without opposition. This was quite an achievement since Unger was a freshman Senator who had beaten a Republican incumbent four years prior. It remains his only race in which he didn't face an opponent.

Thanks to the decennial census, West Virginia had undergone a redistricting process since the last election. Owing to the Eastern Panhandle's expanding population, Jefferson County picked up an additional partial Delegate District to be numbered the 56th. Only one Democrat filed, farmer and nurseryman Bob Tabb. He lost a Primary challenge to Delegate John Doyle in 2000 by three votes out of 2,047 cast. Three Republicans filed for the new seat, all from Berkeley County. Jim Whitacre came out on top with 255 votes, followed by Tom Grove with 235, and Donald Shoemaker with 189. The General Election was quite close, but Tabb won by 113 votes.

John Doyle, who I like to call the "Former, Current, and Future Delegate" was running for re-election to the 57th District and had a close race against Dave Ebbitt, a physician. Ebbitt made tort reform a major part of his platform. Doyle is one of the hardest working campaigners I have ever seen and routinely knocks nearly every door in his district. Clearly it paid off. He received approximately 54% of the vote to Ebbitt's 46%.

Jefferson County's third seat, District 58, had been represented by Dale Manuel since 1989. Fred Blackmer, who had run in the Republican Primary in 2000 ran again and was unopposed. This would be Manuel's last race for the West Virginia House. He tallied 2,353 votes to Blackmer's 1,653.

The Board of Education race was one of the most fascinating elements of the 2002 cycle. Three seats were open, and seven candidates ran. Incumbents Peter Morgens, Pete Dougherty, and Larry Togans all filed for another term. Challenging them were Lori Stilley, Kate Conant, Cheryl Huff, and Delores Milstead. Togans was completing his second term, while Morgens was first elected in 1998. Dougherty had been first elected in 1984, after serving as a Jefferson County Magistrate. Stilley had sought a seat on the Board in 2000, while Milstead was the Democratic nominee for County Commission that year. Conant and Huff were making their first bids for office. 2002 was certainly a change year at the local level and all three incumbents were swept from office, creating a new majority on the Board. Stilley received 2,572 votes, Milstead 2,552, and Huff 2,056. Dougherty came in fourth with 1,569, marking the first election he lost in nearly 25 years of public service. Togans pulled 1,241, Morgens 1,194 and Conant 833.

The massive shift in representation on the Board of Education was the first example of a change coming to Jefferson County politics. It also marked the first time that a majority of members were female, with Stilley, Milstead, and Huff joining incumbent Doris Marshall Cline. Milstead had aligned herself with the slow growth community during her Commission run in 2000. Many of her supporters for that race followed her to the Board race and lined up, too, behind Huff and Stilley. The three ended up running as a slate and this proved to be quite effective. They used the phrase "time for a change" to indicate they wanted to change the direction of the Board. This tactic was replicated by the two eventual Republican nominees for County Commission.

Two County Commission seats were on the ballot, and both were open. Harpers Ferry Commissioner Dean Hockensmith and Kabletown Commissioner Jim Ruland, both Republicans, were retiring after one term of service. Hockensmith, who passed away in 2016, owned and operated Dean's Lawn Mower Shop. According to his obituary he had previously been the manager of H L Mills Gas Station in Ranson, before becoming the supervisor for the Jefferson County Division of State Roads and then a bridge inspector for West Virginia.[1] He was elected in 1996 when incumbent Herb Snyder left the seat to run successfully for the West Virginia State Senate. The Democratic Party nominated Leon Nowrocki, who was killed in a car crash after the primary election. The Democratic Executive Committee then appointed Carol Rockwell who had worked as a guidance counselor in the school system. Her husband, attorney Doug Rockwell, was serving as Party Chair at the time. Hockensmith prevailed. Ruland defeated incumbent Democrat Gary Kable in 1996. While not a county native, he became well known as the owner of RAI Properties and currently owns the Burr Plaza Business Park in Bardane.

Democrats faced a crowded field for both seats when they went to the ballot box. The Harpers Ferry race saw former Ranson Mayor and Charles Town District Commissioner R. Gregory Lance file, after renting property in Bolivar shortly before filing. He has a long record of public service in his family, as his father had served as mayor of Ranson and his mother was a long-time Democratic Party worker. Lance had served two terms on the Commission before being defeated in 1998 by Al Hooper. Richard "Rich" Wilt also threw his hat into the ring. His wife worked in the public school system. The third candidate was, as I stated earlier, my Mom, Mary Everhart Koonce. At the time she was working as a long-term substitute at the Alternative School in Charles Town (now the Martin Delaney Opportunity Learning Center). She had served in leadership with the Young Democrats of Jefferson County, was the vice-president of the Jefferson County Democratic Association, and later the president in the late 90s, and was completing her first term on the Democratic Executive Committee. I always remember her telling me that when she was vice-president of the Democratic Association in the 70s she had planned to run for president when her term was up, but was told that the organization didn't need a woman as president, and thus her service with the group ended until she was asked to join the board again in the 90s.

The Kabletown District race also had three Democrats file. The most well-known was former Board of Education member, teacher, and farmer G. Warren "Jim" Mickey, who had served in leadership positions within the Democratic Party, as had his wife, Reva. Curtis Brannon also filed. Brannon had sought various offices in the 70s, including a seat on the State Democratic Executive Committee and

State Senate. The third candidate was S. Marshall "Steve" Harris, who had a background in law enforcement and would go on to seek office again, both as a Democrat and a Republican.

As I recall the Kabletown Primary was thought to be Mickey's to lose, and he did win by a large margin, receiving 66% to 22% for Harris, and 12% for Brannon. The Harpers Ferry race seemed more muddled, and I'll try to relate my memories as impartially as I can. I know a number of local Democratic officials lined up behind Lance, given his record of public service and experience on the Commission. There was also the perception that he would be the strongest candidate. Wilt had a very well-known last name in the County. While my Mom had been active in a variety of organizations, she had never presented herself as a candidate for office before, except for the Executive Committee. I know she was a bit irritated with Lance's filing, as she had assumed he'd run in 2004 against Hooper for his old seat. I was hesitant to write that, but I know she and Lance had a very good meeting after the primary and they remained on good terms. He had actually been a student of hers when she was student teaching, so they were well acquainted. My Mom set about trying to shore up support from various teachers and school personnel, as well as reaching out to people with whom she had worked in civic organizations who, while regular voters, didn't necessarily consider themselves to be political. She, too, reached out to the "slow growth" activist base, as slowing residential growth was a prime concern for many voters, as it was for her. Not to digress too much, but I will say that I remember a lot of people I'd never met calling and coming to the house to offer support and advice for her campaign—many women, as she was the only woman running for the Commission that year, and had she been elected, she would have been the first Democratic woman on the Commission and only the second overall. In the end, though, she came in second, losing to Lance by less than 100 votes.

I will digress again for a moment. I think I was more heart-broken at her loss than she was. Readers will note that this is typically the habit for me. When I've offered myself up as a candidate and have lost, I move on quite quickly. However, when I truly believe in a candidate and he or she loses, I tend to take it much harder than if I were the actual candidate. In my Mom, and, yes, I know this might be skewed because she was my Mom, I saw a candidate who wanted to make Jefferson County a better and more equitable place to live. I also saw someone who jumped in with both feet, teaching during the day and staying up late at night to brush up on planning ordinances, budgets, and the like, all while continuing to be a parent and a spouse. My Mom readily admitted she probably couldn't have beaten Greg Corliss, the Republican nominee, as he won by a large margin, but I remain skeptical. The Corlisses ended up becoming great friends to me and Greg's wife, Carolyn, and I began a monthly lunch appointment for quite some time.

The General Election seemed even muddier. Residential growth, zoning, and the Planning Commission were big campaign issues. The Republicans, A.M.S. "Rusty" Morgan, III, a farmer and artist who lived in Rippon, and Greg Corliss, a retired Marine Corps General who purchased a small farm in Shenandoah Junction, were both strongly slow growth advocates—though some people will use the term "no-growth." Mickey ran a much more nuanced campaign and favored controls on residential growth, but talked about other issues as well, including infrastructure, the budget, etc. He also spent time discussing the innovation he brought to the Board of Education and the County school system, which he hoped to repeat at the Commission level.

As I stated earlier, Corliss and Morgan ran as a team, and it seemed to pay off. Corliss defeated Lance by 14%, a clearly decisive victory. Morgan's win was much narrower. He took 52% to Mickey's 48%. I know there were County Democrats who supported Corliss and Morgan largely based upon their pledges to ensure there was more oversight relating to residential growth. Further, I know there are some Democrats who felt they would be happy if either Mickey or Morgan won. I do wonder if Lance hurt Mickey's chances, given the margin by which he lost. The Commission continued to be populated entirely by Republicans and with Jim Ruland's retirement, Al Hooper became the Commission President.

In the end 2002 turned out to be a change election at the local level. Jefferson Countians wanted new names and faces and people who were fresh to local politics. It also demonstrated the willingness of many Democrats to support Republicans at the County Commission level based solely upon promises to slow residential growth. This trend would actually turn out to be only a one cycle phenomenon, as some Democratic candidates adopted that rhetoric and picked up strong support from some Republicans because of it.

[1] Obituary of Abner Dean Hockensmith, *Spirit of Jefferson* (Charles Town, WV), May 11, 2016.

6

The Election of 2004

2004 was an interesting year for Jefferson County. Lots of offices were on the ballot, from president on down, and there was interest in just about all the races. This was the election I was most heavily involved in thus far in my life, so I probably have more personal reflections than is decent, so please bear with me.

While I don't typically talk about Presidential Elections in these chapters, I do want to touch upon the 2004 race. I recall my parents, and others, being surprised that George W. Bush won West Virginia in 2000. As I discussed in a previous chapter, Jefferson County (and West Virginia) had been reliably Democratic for generations, with only a few exceptions that typically involved blow out elections for the Republican, like 1972 and 1984. I got the feeling from Democrats on the ground that 2000 was a fluke, and that the eventual nominee would play well in West Virginia in 2004.

Our household was fairly well split. My Dad liked Connecticut Senator Joe Lieberman. My Mom was interested in North Carolina Senator John Edwards and Representative Dick Gephardt of Missouri. I was 100% behind former Ambassador Carol Moseley-Braun, the first

African American woman to serve in the United States Senate. Clearly none of us picked well, as John Kerry won convincingly. While West Virginia's Primary is quite late, I remember most of the interest, locally, being centered around John Edwards and Howard Dean. My Mom's good friend Frances Miller, a former member of the Republican Executive Committee, was totally behind Al Sharpton. Wes Clark had some pockets of support, too, especially from veterans.

I recall hearing about at least two events for Howard Dean in Shepherdstown, one at a private home and another at the Blue Moon, which I attended. I was never really opposed to Howard Dean, but he never made it into my top tier of candidates. I will say, I think he was an excellent Democratic National Committee Chairman, though.

Once the primaries were over, I do recall the Kerry campaign making a modest play for West Virginia. Former United States Senator from Georgia Max Cleland visited Martinsburg to stump for the Kerry/Edwards ticket. Cleland is a Vietnam veteran who lost both legs and an arm in combat. He gave a great speech, and I had my photograph taken with him, which, unfortunately, I gave to someone to enlarge and never got it or the negatives back.

John Kerry, Theresa Heinz, John Edwards, and Elizabeth Edwards all made a joint appearance in Beckley, which I drove down to attend. It was my first time driving that far into the state, alone, and not too terribly long after I got my driver's license. The event was great, although standing on tarmac for three hours in the summer heat wasn't great. I had a sunburn for days afterward!

I must share one other story from this time. There was to be a Young Democrats of America event in DC at Katie Couric's brother's townhouse, featuring some younger members of the United States House. (Yes, random location, I know.) My friend Rod Snyder, who told me about the event, encouraged me to attend. I decided to take the train and I spent the day wondering around DC in 100-degree weather in a suit. I finally got tired of it and went back to Union Station and watched one of the Harry Potter films in the airconditioned movie theater. I promise this story is getting better.

I met Rod at this townhouse, and we found there were only about 10 other people in attendance, which suited me fine, as it wasn't a huge space. The honored guests arrived a few minutes after us and I was able to meet and speak with Representatives Steny Hoyer (MD), Artur Davis (AL), Linda Sanchez (CA), Tim Ryan (OH), and Kendrick Meek (FL). With the exception of Hoyer, all were younger members of the United States House and were part of an effort by House leadership to draw in younger voters. Hoyer is now House Majority Leader. Davis became a Republican and has lost his last few races. Sanchez and Ryan still serve in the US House. Ryan also ran a brief race for President in 2019. Meek was the Democratic nominee for United States Senate in Florida in 2010, coming in third behind Charlie Crist (I) and Marco Rubio (R).

The event was quite nice, and it was fun to meet the members, however I had to catch the train back to Brunswick and I was cutting it close, so I decided to leave. There was only one problem, Representative Sanchez was speaking with another attendee directly in front of the door. I don't really consider myself to be shy, but I wasn't sure of the appropriate protocol when needing to ask a member of Congress to move. So, I waited and loitered until she moved some eight minutes later, making it likely I'd be late for the train. This was probably the last time I jogged in my life, but I did jog back to Union Station only to find I'd missed the last train back to Brunswick.

The first thing I did, which should come as no surprise, was to go to the bookstore in Union Station to purchase a book to read. I decided to get a biography about John Kerry! I then called my parents and explained I needed a ride. So, my Mom had to come get me.

While I waited, I had a very nice read from the book though and began to warm up to Kerry even more. She had lived in Washington after graduating from college and never minded driving in the city. We'll call it an exceptional day, if only for the ability to tell that story.

Neither Senators Byrd nor Rockefeller were facing voters in 2004, but, of course, members of the US House were. Shelley Moore Capito chose to run for a third term. Three Democrats filed in the Primary to face her, Howard Swint, Christopher Turman, and Erik Wells. I'm embarrassed to say I don't remember much about this race except that I was a supporter of Erik. I remember Turman having a family connection to the Eastern Panhandle, but he hadn't lived in the District for long at all. Swint would go on to run again.

Wells is married to Natalie Tennant who was a candidate for Secretary of State and would go on to win the office in 2008. I got to know both of them in '04 and am humbled to call them friends to this day. They had jointly anchored a morning newscast for a number of years and Wells had served in the Navy. He came in third in Jefferson County, but received about twice as many votes as Turman, who was second, across the district.

Incumbent Shelley Moore Capito was unopposed in her Primary, so she and Wells were set to face one another in November. Erik ran a very energetic campaign and crisscrossed the district attending as many parades, fairs, and events as possible. I felt as though he focused on innovation a lot in his campaign—suggesting new solutions for existing problems, rather than just sticking to the established historic talking points of many Congressional issues. Capito did win a second term, but her margin dropped by 3 points. She took 57% of the vote to Wells's 41%. Julian Martin of the Mountain Party received the remaining 2%.

The statewide races featured a couple of open seats. Governor Bob Wise announced he wouldn't seek a second term. Secretary of State Joe Manchin, III, had already declared a challenge to Wise, owing to the revelation that Wise had engaged in an extramarital affair. These moving parts meant no incumbent would be on the ballot for Governor or Secretary of State. All other Board of Public Works officials declared for re-election, Treasurer John Perdue, Auditor Glen B. Gainer, III, Attorney General Darrell McGraw, and Commissioner of Agriculture Gus R. Douglass.

The Secretary of State's race brought out a slew of candidates, most of whom I met and with several of whom I became friends. Those running included former Secretary of State and Congressman Ken Hechler, journalist Natalie Tennant, former WV Treasurer Larrie Bailey, Roger Pritt, Chief Deputy Auditor Donna Accord, attorney and musician George Daugherty, and State Senator Mike Oliverio. In the end Hechler edged Tennant by a few thousand votes and faced banker and businesswoman Betty Ireland in the General Election. In an upset, Ireland won, making her the first woman to be elected to the Board of Public Works, and the second female Secretary of State. She also became the only statewide elected Republican, except for a Supreme Court Justice, who I will get to in a moment.

Although Hechler wasn't the incumbent, I do want to take a few lines to acknowledge his outsized influence, though perhaps forgotten, in West Virginia politics. Hechler was born on Long Island in 1914 and earned several degrees, finishing with a PhD from Columbia University. He taught at a variety of colleges and universities, including Columbia, Princeton, and then Marshall, here in West Virginia. After a tour as a combat historian during WWII, Hechler became a special assistant to President Harry S. Truman (and was rumored to have dated his daughter, Margaret). He worked for a number of government agencies and figures before coming to Marshall to reach political science. He began his service as a member of the United States

House, representing the Fourth Congressional District in 1959 and was re-elected every two years until 1976 when he jumped into the race for Governor, in which he came up short.[1] He then sought his old Congressional seat through a write-in candidacy but was unsuccessful. He again sought the Democratic nomination for his old seat in 1978 but finished second to Nick Joe Rahall. Hechler then worked as a writer, journalist, and professor.[2] In 1984 he was elected West Virginia Secretary of State and served in that role until 2001. He made two more tries for a seat in the United States House, both in 1990 and 2000, but didn't win the Primary in either case. Hechler was the only sitting member of Congress to march with Dr. Martin Luther King, Jr. from Selma to Montgomery in 1965.[3]

I remember meeting Dr. Hechler for the first time at the Jefferson County Fair in 2004. I was lucky enough to have a number of conversations with him over the years and they were always so fascinating. He was well known, too, for campaigning around the state in a red Jeep and his 2004 campaign gave out red Jeep lapel pins as campaign swag. Hechler ran in the Special Election in 2010 for the seat left vacant by the death of Senator Byrd. He died in December of 2016 at the age of 102 and was the oldest living former member of either chamber of Congress at the time.

The Governor's race was fairly interesting. Manchin was joined by a number of candidates including former WV Board of Education President and State Senator Lloyd Jackson and attorney Jim Lees, who had run in 1996 and 2000. Manchin captured over 50% of the vote and Jackson ran second. The main candidates were all fairly moderate to conservative. I had met Manchin a couple of times while he was Secretary of State and I always found him to be warm and a great campaigner. I encountered Jackson and Lees during the Primary, and Senator Jackson and his wife were always very kind to me. I remember they took an interest in younger voters and often would make a beeline for Young Democrats groups. I think this was natural with his concentration on education throughout his career. The statewide name recognition and popularity of the Manchin Family would have made it difficult for any other Democrat to overcome.

Joe Manchin had sought the Governor's chair once before, in 1996, though he lost a close primary to West Virginia State Senator Charlotte Pritt, who had primaried incumbent Democrat Gaston Caperton in 1992. Prior to that he served two terms in the West Virginia House of Delegates (1983-1987) and was a West Virginia State Senator from 1987 until 1997. In 2000 he was elected to the position of Secretary of State, succeeding longtime incumbent Ken Hechler, who retired to run for the United States House. Pritt, State Senator Mike Oliverio, and former Huntington Mayor Bobby Nelson also ran, but Manchin took 51% of the vote. In November of that year he faced no Republican, but Libertarian Poochie Myers, a mystic and artist, did run.

The Republican Primary was just as crowded as the Democratic field. Berkeley County House of Delegates member Larry V. Faircloth, future WV Republican Party Chairman Rob Capehart of Wheeling, South Charleston Mayor Richard Robb, and Monty Warner of Charleston all filed, along with six other candidates. Warner finished first, followed closely by Charleston businessman Dan R. Moore, and then Capehart. Faircloth, however, won Jefferson County.

The November General produced a lopsided result with Manchin tallying 472,758 votes to Warner's 253,131. Mountain Party nominee Jesse Johnson, an actor living in Charleston, polled 18,430 votes. Simon McClure, of Bridgeport, ran a write-in campaign, netting 114 votes across the state. Manchin was considered the foregone winner throughout the run up to the election. Warner highlighted his military service and business background, and Johnson ran to the left of Manchin, but voters seemed comfortable with Manchin's record and he had little trouble winning his first term.

I'll digress here just a bit, as I want to offer some biographical information about Manchin, Johnson, and Wise.

Joe Manchin, III, was born in Farmington, West Virginia on August 24th, 1947. He graduated from Farmington High School and received a B.A. from West Virginia University in 1970. Manchin began the first of two terms in the West Virginia House in 1982 before moving to the West Virginia Senate in 1986, where he stayed for ten years. He was defeated by fellow State Senator Charlotte Pritt in 1996 for the Democratic nomination for Governor. When Secretary of State Ken Hechler announced a run for the US House in 2000, Manchin won both the Primary and General Elections for Hechler's old job. He would later be re-elected as Governor and take a seat in the United States Senate in 2010, where he has served as Vice-Chair of the Democratic Policy and Communications Committee and as Chair of the Committee on Energy and Natural Resources.

This simply wouldn't be a book about West Virginia politics without mentioning some of the more colorful characters I've encountered, one of them being Jesse Johnson. I remember speaking to Johnson in Shepherdstown in 2004, during his run for Governor. He had worked as an actor and I remember him saying he had a part in *Hook*, among other films and shows. I found him to be extremely personable and he had an excellent grasp of the issues and what he hoped to achieve if he was elected. Johnson went on to run for United States Senate and President, while also working as a film maker based in Charleston.

I do want to say a few words about the, then, Governor. I met Bob Wise for the first time at the Old Opera House, where he was greeting local Democrats. He was very friendly and gave a great speech to those in attendance. Over the years of his term, I ran him in a few other times and always enjoyed exchanging a word or two. I had hoped he'd run for a second term, even in light of what might have been an uphill race.

Wise was born on January 6th, 1948, in Washington, DC. He received his law degree from Tulane University School of Law in New Orleans. While practicing law in Charleston, he was elected to the West Virginia State Senate and served from 1980 until 1982.[4] Wise defeated the, then, Senate President, William Brotherton, in the Democratic Primary, thanks in part to heavy support from the West Virginia Education Association. In 1982, he ran for the Democratic nomination for the Third Congressional District. Wise faced G. Kemp Melton and Roger W. Tompkins, both also from Charleston. He was victorious with 26,016 votes to 16,600 for Tompkins and 15,351 for Melton. In the General he defeated incumbent Republican David M. "Mick" Staton by 24,000 votes. Wise would continue to serve the Third Congressional District until the 1990 census caused West Virginia to lose one of its four seats in the US House. The home of Second Congressional Representative Harley O. Staggers, Jr., was drawn into the First District and a portion of the Eastern Panhandle was added to a district that stretched to Charleston. Wise was unopposed in the Primary that year and continued to serve until 2001. In 2000, he sought the Democratic nomination for Governor and faced attorney Jim Lees in the Primary. Wise received 174,202 votes to 101,774 for Lees. The November General was crowded with Wise, incumbent Republican Governor Cecil Underwood, Libertarian Bob Myers, Natural Law Party candidate Randall B. Ashelman of Shepherdstown, and author Denise Giardina of the Mountain Party all on the ballot. Fairmont's Lou Davis also ran as a write-in candidate. Wise barely edged Underwood in Jefferson County, 6,772 votes to 6,598. Statewide results put Wise in the lead with 324,822. Underwood received 305,926, followed by Giardina at 10,416. Underwood would be the last elected Republican governor up until the present day, though Jim Justice, who was elected as a Democrat and switched parties, is currently serving as a Republican.

The Board of Public Works incumbents were all re-elected without much trouble, with one exception. Attorney General Darrell McGraw faced Republican Hiram "Bucky" Lewis, VI, from Morgantown. Lewis has sought political office a number of times since, including most recently a Supreme Court seat in 2018. Lewis won Jefferson County, but came up short statewide by about 6,000 votes, out of over 700,000 ballots cast. I think one of the complicating factors for McGraw was that he wound up running the same year as his brother, Warren, who was seeking another term on the West Virginia Supreme Court. I can't attest to it being an issue, but I can surmise seeing two brothers so closely entwined in the judicial system may have given some voters pause for concern.

Attorney General Darrell McGraw was born in 1936 and is the brother of former Supreme Court Justice Warren McGraw. An army veteran, he served as student body president at WVU. In 1976 he was elected to a 12-year term on the West Virginia Supreme Court of Appeals.[5] He ran for a second term in 1988 but was defeated in the Primary by Thomas B. Miller and Margaret L. Workman, who would go on to become the first female Supreme Court Justice and the first woman to be elected statewide. After leaving the Court, McGraw ran for Attorney General in 1992. The seat was open because incumbent Charlie Brown, who was first elected in 1984, announced his resignation in 1989. Roger W. Tompkins was appointed to the vacant seat and a special election was held in which Mario Palumbo placed first. He opted not to run for a full term, so McGraw faced only Edward Rebrook of Charleston and took 55% in the Primary Election. In the General Election he faced Robert James Gould of Greenville and won a very close race with 52% to Gould's 48%. McGraw had another close race in 1996 against former WV Delegate Charlotte R. Lane, but he faced no opposition in 2000.

The other incumbents fared better. Treasurer John Perdue faced Jefferson County resident Bob Adams in his quest for a third term. I'm not sure where, but I met Adams before he announced his intention to seek office. He's certainly a very personable and friendly person, but our politics couldn't be further apart. It was no surprise that Adams carried Jefferson County, but Perdue won 433,229 to 255,046. I don't recall the size of Adams's campaign operation and Perdue was a popular incumbent, but it's interesting to note it took only two more cycles for the Eastern Panhandle Republican effort to elect a statewide official. Readers can find more about Adams in the chapter about 2008.

John D. Perdue was born on June 22, 1950, in Boone County, West Virginia. After graduating from West Virginia University with a Bachelor of Science degree, he went to work for the State Department of Agriculture and rose to become assistant commissioner. In 1989 Perdue was appointed senior executive assistant to Governor Gaston Caperton and stayed in that position until Caperton left office, at which time Perdue was elected Treasurer. He was also chosen to be President of the National Association of State Treasurers. John and Robin Perdue have two daughters.[6]

Commissioner of Agriculture Gus R. Douglass, who was first elected in 1964, was returned to office. He carried Jefferson County by about 500 votes against Republican Andrew Yost. He also outpaced him across the state tallying 437,881 votes to 253,402. Douglass would be re-elected in 2008, before retiring in 2012 as the longest serving Commissioner of Agriculture in the United States.

State Auditor Glen B. Gainer, III was first elected in 1992, taking over from his father, Glen B. Gainer, Jr., who served from 1977 until 1993. A cousin, Denzil Gainer, had also served as Auditor from 1961 until 1973. In the 1992 Democratic Primary Gainer faced Mark Anthony Manchin, the cousin of then Governor Joe Manchin, who he beat with 63% of the vote. Gainer's 2004 Republican opponent was

Lisa Thornburg, from Milton. Gainer won both Jefferson County and the state, earning 428,177 votes to 267,644 for Thornburg, who had previously worked in the Auditor's Office.

Glen B. Gainer, III, was born on February 26, 1960, in Parkersburg, West Virginia. He obtained a bachelor's degree in political science from the University of Charleston. After graduation he worked for the West Virginia State Treasurer's Office and then John Deere before winning his first time. Gainer and his wife, Susan, have two sons, John and Joshua. He served on a number of boards including as Chairman of the Board of Directors of the National White Collar Crime Center and as President of the National Association of State Comptrollers.[7]

One Supreme Court seat was to be decided this cycle, that of Democrat Warren McGraw, brother of the Attorney General. Justice McGraw has a very long history in West Virginia politics. He served one term in the West Virginia House of Delegates from 1969-1971 and then spent 12 years in the West Virginia Senate, rising to the position of Senate President in his third term. He didn't run for re-election, deciding, rather, to run for Governor in 1984. He faced a number of other well-known Democrats including House Speaker Clyde See, Attorney General Chauncey Browning, and Dusty Rhodes, who was the Highway Commissioner. McGraw came in second to See. Two years later he was elected to the Wyoming County Board of Education and in 1996 won the position of Wyoming County Prosecuting Attorney. After that he was elected to an unexpired term, in 1998, to the Supreme Court, which was set to expire at the end of 2004, which leads us to where we are in the story.[8]

McGraw filed for a full term on the court and faced Jim Rowe, of Lewisburg, in the Democratic Primary. Rowe was, at the time, a Circuit Judge sitting on the 11th Circuit which included Greenbrier and Pocahontas Counties. Rowe had previously been a member of the West Virginia House of Delegates and served two years as majority leader. Governor Gaston Caperton appointed him to a vacancy on the Circuit Court in 1997.[9] I recall Rowe having a reputation as being more conservative than McGraw. Rowe won Jefferson County, but McGraw prevailed overall with 147,030 votes to 112,191 for Rowe.

I remember nothing about the Republican race to take on McGraw. Two candidates filed, Brent D. Benjamin from Charleston and Linda Rice from Huntington. Rice won Jefferson County, but Benjamin edged her out statewide and carried 51,000 votes, not much more than one third of what McGraw won in his primary.

The General Election was fairly nasty. Benjamin defeated McGraw 53% to 47%. Don Blankenship, who we'll hear more from later, invested $3 million in an effort to defeat McGraw. At the time Blankenship was CEO of Massey Energy, which ran the Upper Big Branch mine. Blankenship funneled the money through And for The Sake Of The Kids, which ran ads and paid for mailers attacking McGraw. Massey Energy had an appeal pending for a 1998 case in which Harman Coal was awarded $50 million, to be paid by Massey. The appeal was to be heard by the West Virginia Supreme Court and Blankenship presumably hoped to kick out one justice who he thought might rule against him. The United States Supreme Court eventually ruled that Benjamin couldn't hear any cases involved Massey and a special justice was seated for the appeal.[10] Still, Benjamin was the beneficiary of a full 12-year term. McGraw did jump back into politics by winning the lone Circuit Court seat in the 27th Circuit, which covers Wyoming County. He was re-elected to that position in 2016. His daughter, Suzanne McGraw, is a Family Court Judge for the 13th Family Court Circuit.

Now back to more topical information. There were quite a few local races on the ballot in 2004. The usual every four-year-jobs, State Senate, Assessor, Sheriff, Prosecuting Attorney, Magistrate, plus two County Commission seats and two Board of Education seats. They were joined by the six-year Clerk positions, and the always present House of Delegates seats.

First, perhaps the biggest news of the cycle was the retirement of 36-year incumbent County Clerk John E. Ott. He first entered politics as a candidate for Sheriff in 1960 and 1964, losing the Democratic Primary both times, though by a small margin in '64. The 1968 Democratic nominee, Erma Hough, dropped out of the race for County Clerk and Ott was appointed to run. He only faced opposition once, in 1980, and still won by a wide margin.

I want to digress for a moment, as I have often throughout the book. (And those of you who know me understand I do this all the time!) I've always known who John Ott is. While he's older than my father, his family lived between Halltown and Harpers Ferry, not far from my family's farm. His brother worked for a company my Dad managed and of which he was later majority owner. Another brother served on the Democratic Executive Committee with my Mother, and she knew John from her time working in the Assessor's office. So the name was always familiar. I later became a regular at the Stuck and Alger lunch counter, where John frequently purchased coffee. We talked often, mostly about local politics and County Commission decisions. He's never shy about giving his opinion, but we can disagree agreeably when necessary. I've looked up to him as a public servant, as he was always in his office from 9-5, five days a week, without fail. He worked for the salary the county taxpayers paid him. That example isn't always followed by all of our elected officials in the county or state.

Ott's decision created quite a crowded field. Four Democrats, three of whom had sought County Commission seats in the past, filed and one Republican. 2004 seems to be the year of personal reflections and they continue here. My Dad, Stafford H. Koonce, decided to run, largely at the urging of my Mom. I had pushed her to run, but she said the County Commission had been her only interest. Jeral Milton, an attorney and civic leader, threw her hat in the ring. She had come within a dozen votes of defeating incumbent County Commissioner Gary Kable in the 1996 Democratic Primary for the Kabletown seat. Kable, too, filed for the Clerk's position. The fourth candidate ended up being the nominee, Scott Coyle, the former president of the Jefferson County Planning Commission and a Charles Town Building Inspector. Interestingly, all four came from well-known local families, with only Coyle being a newcomer to politics.

Republican Jennifer Maghan was unopposed for the Republican nomination. A musician, with a younger family, Maghan had a background in management and banking. She also never really emphasized her party affiliation in the General Election, and I sometimes wonder if she wasn't the more liberal of the two, as Coyle can easily be described as a conservative Democrat. While Maghan was new to the County, Coyle's leadership of the Planning Commission during an explosion of residential growth in the county, without a doubt, hurt him with the slow grow reformer community, who had elected Commissioners Greg Corliss and Rusty Morgan two years prior. Maghan's victory did come as a surprise to many residents, and she was the first Republican to hold the seat in at least 100 years.

The other County office races were rather sleepy. Assessor Ginger Bordier drew a Republican challenger for the first time since 1980. Interestingly, her opponent, Jamie Sommers, came to a Democratic event for those interested in running for office. This was Ginger's closest ever and would end up being her last campaign. She took 53% of the vote to 47% for Sommers. Prosecuting Attorney Mike Thompson and Circuit Clerk Patsy Noland were both re-elected without opposition. Sheriff Ed Boober, too, faced no Republican opposition and was re-elected for his second and final term.

The legislative races featured Herb Snyder running for a third term to the WV Senate and incumbent House Delegates Bob Tabb (56th District) and John Doyle (57th District) seeking re-election. Delegate Dale Manuel (58th District) announced his retirement from the House in order to seek one of the two County Commission seats on the ballot, the one held by Al Hooper.

Tabb didn't face a Primary opponent and was able to win a second time against Berkeley County businessman Jim Whitacre. Tabb was just completing his first term and was a natural fit for the rural district, which encompassed part of Berkeley County, as well as part of Jefferson. Whitacre, who lives in Berkeley County, would go on to be elected to the Berkeley County Council.

Doyle did draw a primary opponent, Rod Snyder. Snyder is the eldest son of State Senator Herb Snyder and was making his first run for elective office. At the time he was working in Washington in the agriculture lobbying industry. Both candidates had strong roots in the county. Snyder ran a campaign focused on being a fresh voice in Charleston and did run to the right of Doyle on social issues. In the end Doyle won by a two-to-one margin and went on to face Republican Robert "Bob" Murto from Bakerton, winning by an equally comfortable margin in the General.

Manuel's decision to retire after eight terms created a rare open seat for Delegate in the territory covering Charles Town and Ranson. C. Locke Wysong, Jr., immediately jumped into the race. Wysong had worked for Governor Bob Wise, as his regional representative, was a former president of the Democratic Association, and a well-known and highly regarded Democrat. His mother, Mary "Cesarina" Wysong, who sadly passed away a few years ago, was on the Democratic Executive Committee and a tireless worker for Democratic candidates and causes. She and my Dad were at school together and I had known her since I was in middle school and was very fond of her.

Wysong faced S. Marshall "Steve" Harris in the primary. Harris has a background in law enforcement and had run for County Commission in 2002. On the Republican side Fred Blackmer, the 2002 nominee, filed again, as did Suzanne Morgan, a Republican strategist and consultant. Morgan ran as a center-right Republican and while Blackmer was probably more conservative, he ran a pragmatic race that focused on increasing the efficiency of government and its openness and accessibility to citizens. Morgan won the primary, as did Wysong and they faced off in November. While Morgan did well, Wysong, who is more of a conservative Democrat than Manuel, picked up more support and won by 8%.

The race for State Senate was complicated. Snyder faced Greg Lance in the Democratic Primary. As I wrote in the last chapter, Lance is a former mayor of Ranson and County Commissioner from the Charles Town District. He changed his address to Bolivar in 2002 to run for County Commission from the Harpers Ferry District, and while he won the Primary, he lost the General to Greg Corliss. Snyder ran on his record of two terms in the Senate and touted the fact he was the only chemist in the body. Lance suggested he'd bring new, fresh ideas, and wanted to make the state more business friendly. Lance prevailed by about 500 votes out of over 8,700 cast and faced former WV Senator and later Circuit Judge John Yoder in the General. Yoder had run for office a number of times prior and prevailed with 28,480 votes to 20,748 for Lance. Snyder won the seat back in 2008, when he was in better health, and continued to serve until retiring in 2016. Lance again sought the Harpers Ferry County Commission seat in 2008 and 2018 and ran as the Mountain Party candidate for Sheriff in 2020.

Two County Commission races were on deck this year. Republican Shepherdstown County Commissioner James G. "Jim" Knode announced he wouldn't seek a third term. Charles Town incumbent Al Hooper, also a Republican, chose to run for re-election to a second term. All five Commissioners serving were Republicans at this time, though locally they were thought of as being in three camps. Knode was considered the conservative, while Hooper and Jane Tabb of Middleway were the moderates, and Greg Corliss of Harpers Ferry and Rusty Morgan of Kabletown were the liberals. As best as I can tell, this was almost solely based upon land use issues, impact fees, and appointments to county boards. I wonder given our current climate in the county and Commissioner Tabb's near defeat in the primary of 2018, if any of the other four could be elected as Republicans today.

Jim Knode was first elected to the County Commission in 1992, after having lost the 1986 General Election to incumbent Henry Morrow, Sr. As I recall, he was co-valedictorian of the Class of 1965 from Shepherdstown High School. My Mom always called him "Jimmy," as I suppose that is how he was addressed at school. (She was in the class of 1966.) Knode, who holds an MBA degree, had experience as both a small business owner and business consultant. From reviewing the various campaign ads of 1992 and 1998, Knode ran as a fiscal conservative and campaigned on protecting taxpayer funds.

The race for Charles Town was immediately set once the filing period closed. Hooper would face Dale Manuel in the November General. Two Democrats filed for the Shepherdstown seat, historian Jim Surkamp and retired businessman and Shepherd professor Tom Trumble, who was also a veteran. Former Kabletown County Commissioner and mortgage broker Gary Phalen was unopposed for the Republican nomination.

In Charles Town, Hooper ran on his experience as a commissioner, an engineer, and on his desire to finish some projects he had started, including several with the County Parks and Recreation Department. He also had a tendency to be quite up front and blunt about his position on issues and never danced around his decisions, even if it cost him votes. Manuel ran on his record as an educator and successes in the WV House. While I can't speak for the voters of the county, I think for many this was something of a hard decision as both candidates were very well liked. Manuel did benefit more from the slow growth community than Hooper, even though I recall the Commissioners who were slow growthers supporting Hooper. (I could be wrong about this and will be happily corrected.) In the end Manuel won by his largest margin in a County Commission race, 57% to 43%. Interestingly, Hooper had previously served as County Surveyor, having won election as a Democrat, before becoming a Republican once again. My sense always was that he was part of a now dying breed, the New England Republican.

There wasn't a lot of light between Surkamp and Trumble and many Democrats openly stated they'd be satisfied with either being the nominee. Trumble talked more about his business and military background, while Surkamp hammered historic preservation and sensible planning. I believe Surkamp was better known in the community prior to the Election, and I think that benefited him as he won by a narrow margin. In the General, he defeated Phalen, who indicated he wasn't interested in being as much of a check on residential development as Surkamp. It turned out to be the closest race of the year, 51% to 49%.

With the election of Surkamp and Manuel, the County Commission had its first Democrats since 1998. It had only been 1978 when no Republican had served on the Commission for nearly 120 years. Their election proved to be the first cracks in a dam burst, though perhaps a brief one.

The Board of Education race was a bit of a jolt again in 2004. Two seats were up, those of Paul Manzuk and Doris Marshall Cline. Manzuk had served on the Board for many years and was the pharmacist and owner of Stuck and Alger Pharmacy. Cline retired from the Board Office prior to seeking a seat on the Board several years prior. Manzuk announced plans to retire, while Cline sought another term.

Joining her were Jud Romine, a former Superintendent of Jefferson County Schools, Alan Sturm, retired Assistant Superintendent of Upshur County Schools, and George M. Ganak, who had the support of Stilley, Milstead, and Huff. I also filed for a seat. One of the concerns I heard from a number of voters was the feeling that the current Board or at least a portion of it, was overreaching and not focusing upon increasing staff or student morale. Ganak aligned himself with the three victors from 2002. Cline had joined the majority on a few votes but also differed with them regarding others. While I agreed with some of their goals, I didn't always agree with the process. I did, however, have a blast with the campaign and met some wonderful people.

The voters gave Romine a big section of the vote and he took 4,279 votes to Sturm's 2,970, who edged out Cline for the second seat. She received 2,813 votes. Ganak and I took 1,748 and 1,676, respectively. Voters clearly wanted a check on the Board of Education, but Romine and Sturm would be seated in the minority, having two votes to the three of Stilley, Milstead, and Huff. Romine would go on to resign before the completion of his term.

To this day I believe having younger people in government is important. I was still a teenager when I filed. Additionally, while I hadn't attended a Jefferson County public high school, I had gone to elementary and middle school in the county, thus making me the only candidate that cycle who had been a student in area schools in decades. I enjoyed the candidate forums and meeting people to discuss the issues. I wasn't too terribly surprised that I lost and, in fact, was surprised I did as well as I did.

2004 remains an interesting year for the County. We also saw a snap back from change at the Board of Education level yet continued movement toward a clean slate mentality at both the County Commission and County Clerk level. I will contend we haven't seen a year quite like it since.

[1] "Kenneth William Hechler," History, Art, Archives, The United States House of Representatives, Dec. 20, 2019, https://history.house.gov/People/Listing/H/HECHLER,-Kenneth-William-(H000438)/

[2] Ibid.

[3] James Casto, "Hechler Was Lone Congressman at Montgomery March," *Herald-Dispatch* (Huntington, WV) Mar. 17, 2015.

[4] Robert Ellsworth Wise, Jr., Biographical Directory of the United States Congress, Office of the House Historian, Dec. 24, 2019, https://bioguide.congress.gov/search/bio/W000654.

[5] "November 8, 1936: Darrell McGraw Born in Wyoming County," West Virginia Encyclopedia, Charleston, WV: WVPB, Nov. 8, 2019.

[6] *West Virginia Blue Book.* (Charleston: West Virginia Legislature, 2005).

[7] *West Virginia Blue Book.* (Charleston: West Virginia Legislature, 2005).

[8] *West Virginia Blue Book.* (Charleston: West Virginia Legislature, 2002).

[9] Tina Alvey, "Senior Status Judge James J. Rowe," *Register-Herald* (Beckley, WV) Apr. 24, 2016.

[10] Peter Overby "Massey Energy's Blankenship Has Been Center of Attention Before," The Two-Way, Charleston, WV: WVPB, Apr. 6, 2010.

7

The Election of 2006

I wasn't as involved in 2006 as I had been in 2002 and 2004.
I was busy with classes at Shepherd and had fallen in love with working
at a bookstore in Frederick. I still attended a few events and was kept
up to date by my parents, friends, and the newspapers, but my involvement lessened from the previous cycle.

Senator Robert C. Byrd ran for his ninth and final term in
office. It's hard to be involved in politics in the state and not know
at least a few things about Senator Byrd. At the time of his death in
2010, he was (and remains) the longest serving member of the United
States Senate in history. He is also, as best I can tell, the only West
Virginian to have served in the WV House (1947-1950), WV Senate
(1951-1953), US House (1953-1959), and US Senate (1959-2010). He
served as United States Senate Majority Leader, President pro tempore,
and chairman of the Appropriations Committee. His love of both the
Senate and West Virginia is legendary and needs no restating by me.

Robert Byrd was born Cornelius Calvin Sale, Jr., in Wilkes-
boro, North Carolina on November 20th, 1917. His mother died in the
influenza pandemic of 1918 when he was less than a year old. Per her

wishes he was sent to live with his father's sister, Vlurma Sale Byrd, and her husband, Titus.[1] His name was changed, and he moved to Stotesbury in Raleigh County, a coalmining town. He graduated from Mark Twain High School in 1934 as the valedictorian.[2] Two years later he married Erma Ora James.[3]

Byrd was first elected to office in 1946, while working as a butcher, and he took a seat in the West Virginia House of Delegates, representing Raleigh County, and was re-elected in 1948. In 1950, he moved up to the West Virginia Senate and served a partial term, until December of 1952.[4] Democratic Representative E.H. Hedrick from the Sixth Congressional District announced his intention to run for Governor in 1952 and Byrd jumped into the open Congressional race. The District included Charleston and Beckley and was considered reliably Democratic. He won the seat and was re-elected in 1954 and 1956. Byrd was replaced by John M. Slack in 1958, when he didn't seek re-election. Slack would represent the Sixth District until 1962 when West Virginia lost a seat due to reapportionment. However, he ran and was elected in the Third District and continued to serve until his death in 1980.

In 1958 both United States Senate seats were to be on the ballot. Senator Harley M. Kilgore died in 1956 and West Virginia State Tax Commissioner William Laird, III, was appointed to the vacant seat. A special election was held in which former Republican Senator Chapman Revercomb was elected until 1958. The other seat was due for its regular six-year election and was held by Republican John D. Hoblitzell, Jr., who had been appointed owing to the death of incumbent Matthew M. Neely. Thus, West Virginia had two Republican United States Senators, neither of who had been in office for more than two years.

Byrd opted to seek the seat held by Revercomb, which was for six years. He was elected with 59% of the vote. He won Jefferson and Berkeley Counties and only lost 12 out of 55 counties. The other seat was won by Jennings Randolph with a similar margin. Byrd was re-elected in 1964 with 68% of the vote to Cooper P. Benedict's 32%. Byrd lost only seven counties. His election to a third term saw him win 78% of the vote to Elmer Dodson's 22% and carry every county. Freshman Representative Cleve Benedict challenged Byrd in 1982 but won only one county and 31% of the vote. Six years later State Senator Jay Wolfe challenged Byrd and received 31% of the vote, as well. The Senator faced Stanley Klos in 1994 and again won all 55 counties and 69% of the vote. In 2000 Byrd took 78% to 20% for David Gallaher and 2% for Libertarian Joe Whelan. Senator Byrd ran for an unprecedented ninth term in 2006 and lost only one county to John Raese and lodged 64% of the vote.

I first met Senator Byrd when the Shepherdstown Train Station was rededicated; of course, his reputation preceded him. There were a number of other events at which he spoke or attended where I had the pleasure of hearing him speak, a style which is rarely found in the United States Senate anymore. Owing to his lasting mark on the Democratic Party and, more importantly, the state, the Jefferson County Democratic Party established our annual Senator Robert C. Byrd Democratic Banquet.

Owing to President Bush's victory in 2000 and 2004 in West Virginia, I believe national and state Republicans believed Senator Byrd might be somewhat vulnerable in his quest for another term at the age of 89. Similar efforts to make age an issue had occurred when other older Senators sought re-election, including, most recently, California's Dianne Feinstein. A crowded field of Republicans emerged, though Byrd was challenged in the Primary as well. Billy Hendricks, Jr., of Boone County filed to seek the Democratic nomination, along with Byrd. Hendricks failed to catch on though and lost his home county by 3,022 votes out of 4,422 votes cast.

The Republican field featured six candidates including Hiram Lewis, who challenged Darrell McGraw in 2004, and John Raese, a wealthy media executive who had run for the open United States Senate seat left vacant by Jennings Randolph's retirement in 1984. Raese captured almost 60% of the Primary vote this time and advanced to the November General Election. Joining Byrd and Raese was Jesse Johnson of the Mountain Party. The race was rather unspectacular, and Byrd easily won with 64% of the vote to 34% for Raese and 2% for Johnson. Additionally, Democrats took control of the United States Senate, which made Byrd President Pro Tempore again, as well as Chairman of the Appropriations Committee.

Democrats were enjoying recruitment successes across the country and the precedent of the President's party performing poorly in midterm elections pointed to the possibility of a very good year for Democrats. While Representative Shelley Moore Capito had improved upon her narrow 2000 victory over the past two cycles, Democrats still believed she might be vulnerable as the only Republican member of Congress from West Virginia. Three Democrats vied to face her. Former State Democratic Party Chairman Mike Callaghan, former WV Delegate Mark Hunt, and South Charleston Mayor (and former Republican) Richie Robb all filed. Capito was unchallenged in her primary.

I don't remember a lot about the race, other than many of the local Democrats supported either Callaghan or Robb. Robb, while a former Republican, ran to the left of the other two, from my memory. I met him a couple of times and thought he'd be a good member of Congress. The same with Callaghan. While I would meet Mark Hunt years later, I don't recall encountering him in 2006. The race was fairly close districtwide, but Callaghan enjoyed a larger lead in Jefferson County. He finished with 1,323 votes to Robb's 910, and Hunt's 793. Total votes were Callaghan 19,155, Hunt 16,906, and Robb 15,543. In November Capito again prevailed, both in Jefferson County and in total by about 24,000 votes.

The WV Senate seat held by John Unger, the three WV Delegate seats held by Bob Tabb, John Doyle, and Locke Wysong, along with the Middleway County Commission seat were the only local offices up. All incumbents announced their intentions to run again.

Senator Unger sought a third term and was unopposed in the Primary Election. Jerry Mays was nominated, unopposed, by the Republican Party. Mays served as Chairman of the Berkeley County Republican Party and would go on to be on the West Virginia leadership team for Mitt Romney's 2008 and 2012 bids for President.[5]

As I had stepped back from a lot of activity in local politics, I don't recall many dynamics of this race at all. I didn't, however, run into many people who thought Unger would have a hard time being re-elected. He tallied 19,640 votes to 10,729 for Mays, winning both counties.

All three Delegates covering Jefferson County were fairly easily re-elected this cycle. Bob Tabb (56th District) faced Republican R. Earl Wilbourne, a minister, who lived outside of Summit Point. The 56th District covered parts of Jefferson and Berkeley Counties. Tabb improved upon his margin from 2004 and won both counties with a total of 2,729 votes to 1,837 for Wilbourne. Wilbourne ran a very conservative campaign, but Tabb's reputation as a moderate Democrat with good constituent service prevailed in the rural district. John Doyle was opposed by Republican Bob Murto again. The incumbent received 3,494 votes to the challenger's 2,135. The 58th District saw incumbent Locke Wysong seek a second term and he faced off against 2004 Republican State Treasurer nominee Bob Adams. Wysong was returned to office with 2,876 votes to Adams's 1,840.

Jane Tabb built a reputation amongst both parties as a Commissioner who listened to county residents, weighed the options, and then made a decision. I can't say I agreed with all of her decisions, in fact I strongly disagreed with several, but that's how politics operates. I will say at any point I, or someone in the family, contacted her with a concern or question, she always responded (and still does). While she was well liked, the mood of the county was such that they wanted stronger controls on residential growth and continued to vote for fresh faces in politics.

The only Democrat to file was Frances Morgan of Summit Point. Morgan, an attorney, had worked as a law clerk for Judge Gray Silver, III, and with her husband owned Avanti's Restaurante in Charles Town. Morgan had connections to the county and lived on the farm her family acquired. Her mother, Frances Berry, was also a noted writer in Jefferson County.

If Morgan won, she'd be only the second woman to serve on the Commission and the first Democrat. If Tabb was re-elected, she'd continue as the only woman to ever serve on the body.

I recall supporters of Morgan emphasizing the positive nature of having an attorney as a commissioner, just as supporters of Hooper had with his professional background as an engineer. She also aligned herself with some of the decisions supported by Commissioners Corliss, Rusty Morgan, and Surkamp. I can remember rumors that a few members of the Republican Party leadership supported Morgan quite openly, which created, I'm sure, some uncomfortable discussions at meetings. On Election Day Morgan edged Tabb by 2% and became the first Democratic woman to sit on the body. Democrats now held three of the five seats.

There was quite an assortment of candidates seeking seats on the Board of Education in 2006. Four seats were open. Three four-year terms held by Lori Stilley, Delores Milstead, and Cheryl Huff were to be filled, plus a two-year term held by Sandy Collier, who was appointed when 2004 top vote-getter Jud Romine resigned. In total 12 candidates filled: Cheryl Huff; Sandy Collier; Susan Pellish; Timothy Wayne Hayden; Gary M. Kable; Delores Milstead; Scott Sudduth; Mariland Dunn Lee; Lori R. Stilley; Peter H. Dougherty; JJ Cook; and Ed "Pootie" Johnson.

Dougherty had served for many years on the Board and had been defeated in 2002. Kable was a former County Commissioner and had run, briefly, for County Clerk the previous cycle. They both seemed to have the inside track, given voters' familiarity with their names and previous service. Also gaining attention were Mariland Dunn Lee, a longtime social studies teacher who had recently retired and Scott Sudduth, who had worked on Capitol Hill and for higher education institutions.

There was definitely a push back against the four incumbents from not only the teachers and service employees, but also the general public who, as I saw it, believed there were times when they either made rash decisions or didn't listen adequately to public input or staff prior to making largescale decisions. I had thought it would be hard for all four of them to hold on and in fact they all lost.

Pete Dougherty received the most votes, 4,331, and was followed by Mariland Dunn Lee, 4,094 votes, and Scott Sudduth who took 3,938. They each were seated for a four-year term. Sandy Collier lost her seat, as she took only 1,062 votes. Gary Kable, who came in fourth with 3,457 received the shorter, two-year term and would face voters again in 2008. Huff, Milstead, and Stilley were all defeated, netting 1,023 votes, 891 votes, and 1,035 votes respectively. Pellish received 478, Hayden 402, Cook 473, and Johnson 1,198.

While I'm sure 2006 wouldn't be considered a quiet year for those who were on the ballot or working hard for candidates, I will certainly classify it as a calm before the storm of 2008, when practically every office was on the ballot and most featured a contested Primary.

[1] Adam Clymer, "Robert Byrd, Respected Voice of the Senate, Dies at 92." *The New York Times,* Jun. 28, 2010.

[2] "Robert C. Byrd: A Lifelong Student," United States Congress, http://byrd.senate.gov/issues/byrd_education/byrd_education.html

[3] Adam Clymer, "Robert Byrd, Respected Voice of the Senate, Dies at 92," *The New York Times,* Jun. 28, 2010.

[4] *West Virginia Blue Book.* (Charleston: West Virginia Legislature, 2005).

[5] "Mitt Romney Announces West Virginia Steering Committee, *Romney for President.* Dec. 6, 2011.

8

The Election of 2008

2008 brought a visit by a presidential candidate for the first time in many years. Both parties were facing crowded primaries. (Though those in later years would be even more crowded!) New York Senator and former First Lady Hillary Rodham Clinton visited Shepherdstown on May 7th, 2008, and gave a speech on the steps of McMurran Hall on German Street. She was introduced by University President Suzanne Shipley and endorsed by WV Delegate Bob Tabb, from the 56th District. This was certainly an exciting time for the county.

I had been firmly behind Senator Clinton from the moment she announced. While her stances in 2008 were a touch more moderate than my personal beliefs, I believed she had the experience, strength, and intelligence to be a wonderful President. I, too, believe it has long since been time for a woman to be President of our country.

While it may be unpopular for me to declare, I think a visit by just about any presidential candidate to an area is cause to celebrate. I will draw the line when that candidate espouses vitriol or hateful speech and I need go no further with that explanation. So, if Senator Obama had visited the county, I would have been pleased as well.

There were quite a few supporters of Senator Obama, as well, and they were largely respectful, though, at times, holding up large cardboard signs which made it difficult for those in the back to see well. Senator Clinton gave a very nice speech and then took time to greet some of the attendees. I'm sorry I didn't get a photograph with her, but I was able to shake her hand, and I took a couple from the crowd.

Both of West Virginia's Senators endorsed Senator Obama over Senators Clinton and Edwards. Whether it's true or not, I've always heard that Senator Byrd wasn't much of a Bill Clinton fan owing to his extramarital dalliances. In part Byrd said, "Barack Obama is a noble-hearted patriot and humble Christian, and he has my full faith and support."[1] Rockefeller's endorsement came earlier in the year and included mention of Obama's judgment on national security matters and the Iraq War.[2] Even with the support of both Senators, Obama only received 92,736 votes in West Virginia, while Clinton tallied 240,890. The votes in Jefferson County were: 4,344 for Senator Clinton, 4,039 for Senator Obama, and 399 for Senator Edwards.

As I've said before, owing to our late Primary date, the Presidential Primary Elections are usually decided by the time we vote, as was the case with the 2008 Republican Primary. Arizona Senator John McCain was already the de facto nominee and he received 90,469 votes to 12,310 for former Arkansas Governor Mike Huckabee, 5,969 for Texas Representative Ron Paul, and 5,242 for former Massachusetts Governor Mitt Romney.

The November result nearly mirrored the 2004 Presidential Election with John McCain winning West Virginia and receiving 397,466 votes to 303,857 for Barack Obama and 7,219 for Ralph Nader.

However, Obama did win Jefferson County by approximately 1,000 votes. He became the last Democrat to win a Presidential race in Jefferson County to date.

Senator Jay Rockefeller was seeking what would be his final term in office. He was first elected in 1984, after serving two terms as Governor and one as Secretary of State. Rockefeller was opposed in the primary by former Republican WV Delegate Sheirl Lee Fletcher and Byrd's 2006 Primary opponent Billy Hendricks, Jr. The result was a blow out for Rockefeller, as he won 271,425 votes to Fletcher's 51,073, and Hendricks's 29,707. M. Jay Wolfe, a former WV State Senator, was unopposed for the Republican nomination. Wolfe had run against Senator Byrd in 1988 and Rockefeller in 2002. While the raw number of votes increased over 2002, the percentages were about the same with Rockefeller winning approximately 64% again.

As 2008 felt like another good year for Democrats, an effort was launched again to attempt to dislodge Shelley Moore Capito from her Second Congressional District seat in the US House. Three Democrats filed, Anne Barth, Richie Robb, and Thornton Cooper. John Unger had mulled a challenge to Capito and seemed like he'd be a very strong candidate, given his base of support in the Eastern Panhandle, but he opted against making the challenge. Barth was a long serving aide to Senator Byrd and had worked as his state director. She was considered to be the strongest challenger to Capito to date. Robb had run in 2006 and was the longtime Mayor of South Charleston. He had run as a Republican for WV Supreme Court and Governor. Cooper had made several runs at state legislative seats and was based in Charleston. Barth emerged victorious from the Primary with 63% of the vote to 29% for Robb and 8% for Cooper.

In the General Election, Byrd pushed very hard for Barth, as did national Democratic groups. Of note is that this was the first time in the history of West Virginia elections that both major party nominees were women. Had Barth won, she would have been only the second Democratic woman to represent West Virginia in Congress and just the third overall. She did win Jefferson County by 18 votes (yes, 18 out of 22,000 cast), but she lost district-wide, receiving 43% of the vote to Capito's 57%. Many consider this to be the last serious challenge Capito received for her seat in the House.

Governor Joe Manchin sought a second term. He was opposed in the Primary by former WV Delegate Mel Kessler, who tallied 25%. Russell E. Weeks, Jr., was unopposed for the Republican nomination. Weeks had run for the West Virginia Senate in 2002 and defeated Bill Wooton, the powerful chairman of the Senate Judiciary Committee, in an upset. He was subsequently defeated in 2006 when he sought a second term. The Mountain Party nominated 2004-nominee Jesse Johnson again. Manchin was easily re-elected and became the first Governor since Gaston Caperton in 1992 to be re-elected to a second term. He received 70% of the vote. Weeks took 26% and Johnson 4%.

Incumbent Republican Secretary of State Betty Ireland surprised many by announcing that she wasn't seeking a second term in office. I remember lots of people, on both sides of the aisle, suggest that she would be a formidable challenger to Governor Manchin or Senator Rockefeller. In the end she didn't seek any office in 2008. On the Democratic side, 2004 candidate Natalie Tennant filed. She had come very close to a first-place finish but was edged out by former Secretary of State Ken Hechler. Tennant faced two other Democrats, Joe DeLong, the WV State House Majority Leader, and WV State Senator Billy Wayne Bailey, Jr. Tennant prevailed, earning 51% of the vote, followed by DeLong at 36% and Bailey at 13%. The Republicans nominated Charles Minimah, the first African American nominee by either major party for Secretary of State.

I've often thought of Betty Ireland as a rather interesting elected official. I met her in 2004 when she stopped by to campaign in Jefferson County. I appreciated seeing her on Rt. 340 putting up her own campaign signs and her pledge to modernize the Secretary of State's office. Ireland was born in Charleston in 1945 and first worked as a teacher before transitioning to the business world, focusing on banking and pensions. She was elected to a four-year term on the Charleston City Council in 1987. In 1998 she began a four your tour as the executive director of the West Virginia Consolidated Retirement Board. Ireland wouldn't seek re-election in 2008 but did enter the special election for Governor in 2011, coming in second in the Republican Primary to Bill Maloney.[3] I have heard that she has since left the Republican Party, but this isn't confirmed.

No matter who won, Tennant or Minimah, history was to be made in West Virginia. Minimah would have been the first African American elected to statewide office in West Virginia and the first non-judicial African American statewide official in the state. Tennant would have been the first Democratic woman elected to a non-judicial statewide office and the first woman to succeed another woman for a statewide office in West Virginia. When the votes were all counted Tennant received 66% to Minimah's 34%.

John Perdue, Glen B. Gainer, III, and Darrell McGraw were all unopposed in their primaries for another term as Treasurer, Auditor, and Attorney General, respectively. Gainer and Perdue faced no Republican opponents and were, thus, re-elected without opposition.

There was a contested primary for the Republican nomination for Attorney General, between Daniel W. Greear and 2004 nominee Hiram Lewis. Greear prevailed with 53,121 votes to Lewis's 42,426. McGraw had a very close re-election race, winning by only half a percent. This would be his last term in office, and I cover more about him in the chapter about the 2012 Elections.

The race for Commissioner of Agriculture drew a contested primary on both sides. Longtime Democratic incumbent Gus R. Douglass was opposed by Oscar Wayne Casto in the Primary. Douglass won 193,766 votes to Casto's 113,400. On the Republican side James Michael Teets and Lawrence T. Beckerle competed. Teets became the nominee by winning 65% of the vote. Douglas had been in office for four decades, with one four-year break, and both his primary opposition and Republican opponent suggested it was time for a change. The voters of West Virginia disagreed though and returned him to office with 53% of the vote. This was his closest race to date.

Two Supreme Court seats were on the ballot this cycle. Incumbents Margaret Workman and Elliot "Spike" Maynard both opted to run again. Maynard was considered a very conservative Justice, from what I recall, and there was some question as to whether or not he would be able to win the Primary. That thought came to be true as he was a distant third in the Primary voting. Workman won 180,599 votes, followed by attorney Menis Ketchum with 135,563. Maynard received 97,409. WVU Law Professor Bob Bastress tallied 88,490 votes. Maynard would go on to switch his party affiliation to Republican and run for Congress in the Third District in 2010.

Only one Republican, Beth Walker, filed for the Supreme Court, so she was guaranteed a place on the General Election ballot. Surprisingly, Ketchum came in first with 355,778 votes, followed by Workman with 336,346. Walker was very close behind and took 329,395 votes, nearly defeating Workman. With the victories of Workman and Ketchum, the Court remained 4-1 in Democrats' favor, with Justice Brent Benjamin as the lone Republican.

Incumbent WV State Senator John Yoder decided against running for another term. Former WV Senator Herb Snyder filed and was unopposed in the Primary. County Commissioner Rusty Morgan announced his intention to run on the Republican ticket, but he withdrew from the race. Bob Adams, who had run for WV Treasurer in 2004 and WV House in 2006 also filed. Morgan remained on the ballot but didn't actively campaign and had announced that he was no longer seeking the seat. Still, he polled 30% of the vote to Adams's 70%.

Snyder, who was seeking a return to the State Senate after losing the Democratic Primary in 2004, laid out the goals he wished to accomplish if he was able to return and emphasized his professional background as the only chemist who might be serving in 2009. The expansion of Route 9 increased educational funding, and more jobs were hallmarks of his campaign. Snyder also said his health was greatly improved and he was ready to return to work.

Adams, who I knew from my time commuting to Washington, DC, focused on his background as a Navy veteran and small business owner. At one point he worked for the Office of Public Affairs for the American Legislative Exchange Council. He said his campaign was based around wanting "the next generation of West Virginians to have better opportunities for a quality education, good-paying jobs, and affordable healthcare."[4]

Delegates Bob Tabb (56th) and John Doyle (57th) filed for reelection. 58th District Delegate Locke Wysong announced his retirement, leaving an open seat. Tabb and Doyle were unopposed in the Democratic Primary. The Republican Party didn't field a challenger to Tabb. Betsy Dungan, daughter of Gary and Anne Newcomer Dungan, sought the Republican nomination for the 57th. Dungan's parents were very active in the county and state Republican Party. Anne was the Republican nominee for this seat in 2002 and Gary was the Republican nominee for Assessor this year, as well. Betsy Dungan had been a student at Shepherd and was fairly young in comparison to the typical age of political candidates.

Wysong was first elected in 2004, taking over from Democrat Dale Manuel, who was elected to the County Commission. Two Democrats filled for the seat, Tiffany Lawrence, a public relations executive and member of the Democratic Executive Committee, and Richard C. Watson. Lawrence had previously been crowned as Miss West Virginia and traveled the state in that role. No Republican filed in the Primary. Lawrence received 65% of the vote to Watson's 35%. The Republican Party appointed Tomas Engle to the vacant ballot line for the November General Election.

All of the Circuit Judge seats were up this cycle as well. This would turn out to be the last time regular elections for this office were partisan. Since the previous election in 2000, a fifth division had been added and Gina M. Groh had been appointed by Governor Manchin. She, along with the other incumbents who chose to run, now had to compete for new eight-year terms. The seats are divided up into divisions, but this doesn't have anything to do with residency.

The Division 1 seat was held by Judge David H. Sanders, who was first elected in 1992, as a Democrat. He opted to run again for another term and was unopposed in the Primary and drew no Republican challenger in the General. The Division 3 seat was held by Republican Judge Christopher C. Wilkes, who was also elected in 1992 and who remained the lone Republican judicial official covering Jefferson County for quite some time. He faced no opposition in the Primary or General Elections. The Division 4 seat was held by Democrat Gray Silver, III, who had squeaked by in the 2000 Primary for this new seat. He faced no opposition and was re-elected this cycle. Division 5 saw Judge Groh run for a full term as a Democrat. Republican Harry Patton Waddell also filed.

Groh defeated Waddell and, in so doing, became the first elected female Circuit Judge in the Eastern Panhandle. It is rather hard to believe that until she was appointed in 2006 no woman had been a Circuit Judge in the Panhandle, and few had done so across the state.

The Division 2 seat was a little more complicated. Judge Thomas W. Steptoe, Jr., decided to retire after serving 24 years on the bench. He had previously been a member of the House of Delegates from 1981-1985, representing Jefferson County. Two Democrats and one Republican filed. The Republican, State Senator John C. Yoder faced no opposition and advanced to the General. The Democratic race was between Berkeley County attorneys Michael Lorensen and Michael Santa Barbara. Lorensen was victorious with 11,013 votes to Santa Barbara's 7,993.

An additional Family Court seat was added for the 2008 election. The two incumbent Democrats, Sally Gavin Jackson and William Wertman were unopposed in the Primary and General. The new seat was won by Democrat David Greenberg, without opposition.

I feel like I always start with the County Commission races, but they are often the most interesting. Commissioners Greg Corliss from Harpers Ferry and Rusty Morgan from Kabletown were both ending their first terms and neither planned to run again. Morgan, though, opted to jump into the WV Senate race, but more on that later.

The Harpers Ferry seat drew quite the crowd. Former Charles Town County Commissioner Greg Lance, planner Lyn Widmyer, and businessmen Ed Burns and Steve Pace all planned to run on the Democratic side. I covered Lance before in previous chapters, but in summation, he is a former mayor of Ranson and County Commissioner from Charles Town. He was the Democratic nominee for WV Senate in 2006 and ran a strong campaign but came up short. Truth be told, I think his interest has always been in the County Commission. Burns and Pace were both new to local politics.

Widmyer, who retired as the Parks and Trail Planning Supervisor with the Montgomery County Parks Department, had been active in a wide variety of civic organizations over the years, including the Jefferson County Fair and the League of Women Voters. Her husband, Ron Widmyer, who interestingly enough was a groomsman in my parents' wedding, trained as an engineer and taught at Shepherd while running the family farm and other properties. She ran under the slogan "Win with Lyn."

Lance was probably the best known of the four, owing to his previous experience in politics. Widmyer would have been a close second, while Pace and Burns worked to increase their name ID. Lance appeared in ads with Kabletown candidate Patsy Noland and, again, seemed to have support from the real estate and construction communities. Widmyer made planning a central theme of her campaign and received support from many of the voters who propelled Frances Morgan to victory two years prior. She won convincingly with 48% of the vote, followed by Lance at 30%, Burns at 17%, and Pace at 5%.

An Independent candidate jumped in as well, Paul Ashbaugh, a resident of the Blue Ridge. Ashbaugh is both a developer and builder who had quite the following in the County. He had repeatedly testified against impact fees and restrictions on development at various public hearings. He had the strong backing of people from the building and development industry.

No Republican filed for the seat and the Republican Executive Committee nominated Melodie Williams for the ballot line, thereby creating a three-way race.

The battle lines relating to residential development appeared again in 2008. Much like 2002, 2004, and 2006, proponents of impact fees, a strengthened plan for future growth, and diversification of appointments to Jefferson County boards came out in force, as did those favoring little to no controls on growth. Widmyer and Ashbaugh were the most active campaigners and it struck me that Williams was sort of lost in the shuffle and probably benefited mostly from voters who simply voted straight Republican. Widmyer prevailed with 45% of the vote, followed by Ashbaugh at 28%, and Williams with 27%.

The race for the Kabletown seat was much less crowded. Circuit Clerk and former Magistrate Patsy Noland announced her intention to run. She had served as Magistrate from 1984 until 1994, and then as Circuit Clerk since 1994. Joining her in the Democratic field was Kit McGinnis, who ran to the left of Noland. McGinnis's background was in non-profit management and sustainable development. She was definitely closer on the issues to Commissioners Morgan, Corliss, Morgan, and Surkamp than Noland. In the end, Noland's decades of electoral successes no doubt assisted her, as did her connections within the community and she prevailed over McGinnis, tallying 4,942 votes to McGinnis's 3,101, and faced Republican Frank Kubic in the November General.

The General Election wasn't particularly active. I don't recall Kubic doing much in the way of campaigning. He didn't appear in the local Republican Party's voters' guide, which was unusual. I know he was a Navy veteran and had worked for IBM, but I remain unsure as to where he fell on the issues. It seemed a foregone conclusion that Noland would win, and she did, taking 63% of the vote.

With the election of Widmyer and Noland, the County Commission now had a female majority, as they joined Commissioner Frances Morgan. Additionally, the other two Commissioners, Dale Manuel and Jim Surkamp, were both Democrats, meaning the Commission had shifted from five Republican members in 2004 to five Democrats in 2009.

2008 marked a few high-profile departures from county government. Incumbent Sheriff Ed Boober was term limited, having served since 2001. Long time Prosecuting Attorney Mike Thompson, who was first elected in 1984, decided to retire, as did Assessor Ginger Bordier, who had been re-elected every four years since 1980. All three races drew a contested Democratic Primary and Republicans put forth a candidate for Sheriff and Assessor.

There was something of a tradition in Jefferson County for the Assessor to be someone who had worked, for some time, in the office, prior to serving. Incumbent Ginger Bordier and her predecessor Kathryn Trussell had both done so. This year was no different. While four candidates filed, only one had been employed by the office, Angie Banks. She was joined by Sheriff Ed Boober, former Jefferson County Surveyor John Kusner, and Jerri Herbert. This was Banks's first bid for office, as it was Herbert's. Boober had been the Democratic nominee for the Middleway County Commission seat in 1994 and was twice elected Sheriff. Kusner had run for the County Commission, as well, and had been elected as Surveyor several times. Banks worked tirelessly, knocking on doors and reaching out to voters. She emphasized her experience in the Assessor's Office and the lack of on-the-job training that would be needed. Boober, too, had a background in county government and the Sheriff also serves as the official Treasurer for the County. When the votes were all counted Banks was nominated with 39% of the vote. Boober was a close second with 35%, followed by Kusner at 15%, and Herbert at 11%.

In the November General Election, Banks would face Republican nominee Gary Dungan, who had run unopposed. Dungan was very active with the Jefferson County and West Virginia Republican Parties. His wife, Anne Newcomer Dungan, had been the Republican nominee for the West Virginia House from the 57th District in 2002. He was a retired banker and member of the Jefferson County Development Authority. Dungan played up his experience in finance, while

Banks continued to point out her familiarity with the office and its business. Out of over 20,000 votes, Banks took 11,959 or 57% to Dungan's 8,890 votes. With Banks's victory, she added to the trend of the position of Assessor being the longest stretch of a countywide office solely being occupied by a woman.

The race for Sheriff featured three candidates, all of whom had law enforcement backgrounds. Bobby Shirley, Louis Brunswick, and Gerald Koogle, all threw their hats into the ring. Sheriffs in West Virginia are only permitted to serve only two consecutive terms, although they may opt to run again after a break between their second term and a future third term. Shirley was a longtime employee of the Jefferson County Sheriff's Department and had served on the County Parks and Recreation Committee. I recall my Mom saying he always wanted to be Sheriff, though I'm not sure if this is true. If so, I suspect he made career moves to ensure his viability. Brunswick had retired as the Chief of Police for Charles Town and would have been the first African American Jefferson County Sheriff, if he was elected. Koogle had spent 18-years with the Frederick, Maryland Police Department.

I opted to support Brunswick in this race. I thought he had the temperament and experience to be an outstanding Sheriff for Jefferson County. At the time I had nothing negative to say or think about Shirley, and I had known him for quite some time, but I just thought Brunswick was a better fit. A majority of the voting Democrats didn't agree with me, though, and Shirley took 51% to 34% for Brunswick, and 15% for Koogle.

The race for Sheriff was one of the few to be contested in the Republican Primary. Two men filed for the position, Brian Parrish and Jay Watson. Watson easily won with 70% of the vote. He served for decades with the Fairfax County Fire and Rescue service and had been the chaplain for the Ranson Police Department. I remember several Democrats indicating they liked Watson a lot and lamented that he was running as a Republican. Watson received 41% to Shirley's 59% and the office remaining in the hands of the Democratic Party.

Ralph Lorenzetti, a longtime assistant prosecuting attorney, threw his hat into the ring for Mike Thompson's seat. Also filing was Ruth McQuade of Shepherdstown. The tenth of 15 children, McQuade grew up in Richwood, West Virginia, worked as an Assistant Attorney General in West Virginia, and then as a federal prosecutor for two decades.[5] Both candidates had relevant experience for the job. I do remember McQuade suggesting she would be a tougher prosecutor. Although residential growth wasn't really an issue that could be controlled by the Prosecuting Attorney, a lot of the same people who supported slower growth candidates also lined up behind McQuade. Lorenzetti was quite well known throughout the county, as was his wife, Dr. Rosie Cannarella. He received the nomination after taking 54% of the vote to McQuade's 46%. Since no Republican ran and the Republican Committee didn't appoint a candidate, Lorenzetti automatically became Jefferson County Prosecuting Attorney in January of 2009.

The incumbent Magistrates, Mary Paul Rissler, Gail Boober, and Bill Senseney ran unopposed in the Democratic Primary and no Republican candidates ran, thus ensuring they were all returned for another four years.

Almost as quiet as the race for Magistrate, the Board of Education had two seats for voters to fill and incumbents Gary Kable and Alan Sturm but filed again. They were joined by one other candidate, Buster Nicholson. Both incumbents were re-elected without much trouble.

As 2008 closed, it was certainly a good year for Democrats in Jefferson County, but the pendulum was set to swing once again.

[1] Paul Nyden, "Byrd Endorses Obama for President," *Charleston Gazette* (Charleston, WV) May 19, 2008.

[2] "Rockefeller Endorses Obama," *Herald-Dispatch* (Huntington, WV) Feb. 29, 2008.

[3] "Betty Ireland," *The West Virginia Encyclopedia*, WV Humanities Council, Dec. 7, 2015, https://www.wvencyclopedia.org/articles/2330.

[4] "Selection 2008," Jefferson County Republican Party (Charles Town, WV), Sept. 1, 2008.

[5] "Local Attorney to Run for Commission," *Shepherdstown Chronicle* (Shepherdstown, WV) Nov. 20, 2019.

9

The Election of 2010

Before I launch into the usual discussion of this year's Elections, it is important to note that Senator Byrd died on June 28th of 2010. His passing truly left a hole in the United States Senate, the Democratic Party, and West Virginia. A special Primary Election was called, with the General Election to coincide with the regularly scheduled one.

In the meantime, Carte Goodwin was appointed to the vacant seat and announced he wouldn't run to fill out the two years remaining of it. When seated he became the youngest United States Senator serving at that time. Goodwin is an attorney in Charleston and had been on staff for Governor Manchin. Jefferson County had the honor of hosting him as the speaker at our first Senator Robert C. Byrd Democratic Dinner.

Carte P. Goodwin was born in Mt. Alto, West Virginia on February 27, 1974. He received his B.A. from Marietta College and his J.D. from Emory University School of Law in 1999. After clerking for the Fourth Judicial Circuit of the United States Court of Appeals, Goodwin engaged in the private practice of law until he became General Counsel to Governor Manchin from 2005 until 2009. He served in the United States Senate from July 16th until November 15th of 2010. He is married to Rocky Goodwin, Senator Rockefeller's former State Director, and is a cousin to 2016 Democratic Gubernatorial candidate Booth Goodwin.[1]

The Special Primary Election took place on August 28th, 2010. Three Democrats filed, 10 Republicans, and one Mountain Party candidate. Governor Joe Manchin ran in the Democratic Primary and faced former Representative and Secretary of State Ken Hechler and former WV Delegate Sheirl Lee Fletcher. Hechler ran far to Manchin's left and made his opposition to mountain top removal mining a hallmark of his campaign. At 96, Hechler would have been the oldest Senator serving. I've covered Hechler previously in the book, but I do want to take a few moments to discuss Delegate Fletcher.

At the time of this election Sheirl Fletcher was based in Morgantown and owned Fletcher Environmental Services. She was first elected to the West Virginia House of Delegates in 1998, interestingly as a Republican, and was re-elected in 2000. After changing her party registration to Democrat in 2003, she filed in the 2008 United States Primary against Jay Rockefeller.[2] From what I can remember she ran to Manchin's right, though they largely agreed on energy policy.

When the votes were tallied, Manchin pulled in 68,827 to 16,267 for Hechler, and 9,108 for Fletcher. Manchin won all 55 counties in the state. 2010 became the first year since 1956 in which the Democratic nominee for a United States Senate seat from West Virginia wasn't Jennings Randolph, Robert Byrd, or Jay Rockefeller.

The Republican race featured some familiar names. John Raese, who had challenged Byrd in 2006 filed, as did Andrew Warner, brother of 2004 Republican candidate for Governor Monty Warner, and Frank Kubic of Jefferson County, who was the Republican nominee for the Kabletown County Commission seat in 2008. Raese received 71% of the vote to 15% for Warner and the rest scattered.

Manchin received heavy support from the labor movement, especially the United Mine Workers of America. His campaign remarks often featured the need to ensure working West Virginians had the support and opportunities they deserved. Raese favored a quite conservative platform which including eliminating the minimum wage. They were joined by two third party candidates. Jesse Johnson was again nominated by the Mountain Party and Jeff Becker received the ballot line of the Constitution Party. Johnson ran to the left of Manchin and Becker to the right of Raese.

I always found it somewhat shocking that Raese actually led Manchin in some public polling during the race. 2010 was, of course, a disastrous year for Democrats across the country and I suppose some of Raese's energy came from those currents. The election was the closest Senate race since Senator Rockefeller's first-term victory in 1984, interestingly also against Raese. Manchin received 53%. Raese received 43%, Johnson 2%, and Becker 1%.

As I indicated earlier, 2010 was a disastrous year across the country for Democrats and it wasn't too good here at home. Not many offices were on the ballot this cycle. The usual US House seat was up, as well as one State Senate seat, three State House seats, a special election for Supreme Court Justice, two County Commission seats, and the County Clerk and Circuit Clerk positions.

Only one Democrat filed to take on Shelley Moore Capito for the US House seat this year, Jefferson County's own Virginia Lynch Graf. Ginny Graf and her husband became active with local Democratic politics around 2004. I remember meeting them at some local meetings and she restarted the Organization of Democratic Women in Jefferson County, which flourished under her leadership. A former nun, Graf made social justice issues the backbone of her campaign, as I saw it. She ran a very spirited effort with the theme of being willing to "stick her neck out" and go against the grain to support the needs of West Virginians. Capito was re-elected with 68% of the vote to Graf's 30%. Constitution Party nominee Phil Hudok received 2% of the vote. It should be noted that 2010 was only the second time in the history of West Virginia that both major party nominees for a federal election were women, the first being 2008.

I do wish to touch upon the other two United States House seats in West Virginia for a moment. Longtime incumbent Alan Mollohan, who had represented the First District since 1983 was defeated in the Democratic Primary by State Senator Mike Oliverio. Oliverio was then, in turn, defeated in the General Election by David McKinley. Mollohan's loss meant a majority of West Virginia's Congressional seats were held by Republicans for the first time since 1949. Nick Joe Rahall, the incumbent Democrat in the Third District had a much closer race than usual. He faced former Democratic Supreme Court Justice Spike Maynard, who had become a Republican after he was defeated in his re-election bid for the Court. The race was 56% for Rahall to 44% for Maynard, closer than his last few re-election bids. It would take another two cycles before all three United States House seats in West Virginia were occupied by Republicans.

In 2008, former Supreme Court Justice Thomas McHugh was appointed by then-Chief Justice Spike Maynard to step into the seat held by Justice Joseph Albright, who took a medical leave of absence. Unfortunately, Albright died the next year and Governor Manchin appointed McHugh to serve until a special election could be held. The term only ran until the end of 2012 and McHugh pledged to only serve until then, if re-elected. No other Democrats filed for the Special Election this year. One Republican did, Jefferson County Circuit Court Judge John Yoder.

Yoder was the Republican nominee for the United States Senate in 1990, losing to Senator Rockefeller. He was then elected to the West Virginia State Senate, in 1992, and served until 1996. In 2002 he ran for the Jefferson County Commission but placed second in the Republican Primary to Greg Corliss. He was again elected to the State Senate in 2004, but didn't seek re-election, instead winning a Circuit Court seat, which he held until his death in 2017. 2010 would be the closest he came to winning a seat on the Supreme Court. McHugh received 51% of the vote to Yoder's 49%.

2010 brought a number of primary challenges to Democrats in our area. Senator John Unger filed for another term and was challenged in the Democratic Primary by Patrick Hale Murphy, who had served in the West Virginia House, on the Berkeley County Commission, and the Berkeley County Board of Education. Unger prevailed with 4,073 votes to Murphy's 1,784 and advanced to the November General Election to face Republican member of the House of Delegates Craig Blair, who had been unopposed in his Primary. 2010 would prove to be Unger's closest race. He squeaked by with 50.4% of the vote to Blair's 49.6%.

The 56th District, which had been held by Bob Tabb since its creation in 2002 had a new face as an incumbent. Tabb resigned from the seat in 2009 to take a position as Deputy Commissioner of Agriculture. Since the seat was held by a Democrat, the Democratic Executive Committee was charged with submitting the name of a suitable replacement. Terry L. Walker, a Kearneysville native and real estate agent, was selected for the seat and appointed by the Governor. Walker, therefore, became the first African American legislator from the Eastern Panhandle. He filed to run for a full term and Inwood businessman Eric L. Householder was the lone Republican candidate. Interestingly they both have the middle name Lee. As the 56th District was the most conservative in the County, Walker ended up falling short. He took 44% of the vote to Householder's 56%. Householder became the first Republican to represent part of Jefferson County in the House in several generations.

Incumbent Democrat John Doyle of the 57th District faced a Primary challenger for the first time since 2004, Lorraine "Lori" Rea. She focused much of her campaign rhetoric on a perceived like of friendliness toward business on the part of West Virginia. I do believe she ran to Doyle's right overall. Doyle won the nomination again with 65% of the vote. Two Republicans competed to face him in November, Elliot Simon and Donald Anthony Jones. Simon emerged with roughly the same percentage of his Party's vote as Doyle received from his. In the General the incumbent was re-elected by about 8 percentage points.

The race for the 58th wasn't as crowded. Tiffany Lawrence filed for a second term and was unopposed in the Primary. Her Republican opponent, Alan Blake Thompson, was likewise unopposed. This was the one race in which I don't remember hearing a peep out of the Republican. I suppose part of it was based upon the fact that I didn't live in the 58th District. Lawrence was re-elected to a second term, receiving 53% of the vote.

A couple of offices were to be filled in the Primary Election of 2010. One of the Conservation District Supervisor positions was open, and Bobby Gruber was elected unopposed. Three seats on the Board of Education were also to be filled, in what was a much more sedate affair than some of the other recent Board of Education races.

The three incumbent members, Scott Sudduth, Pete Dougherty, and Mariland Dunn Lee all filed to retain their seats. Joining them on the ballot were Karan Townsend, who owned a bed and breakfast in Harpers Ferry and physical therapist and parent Laurie Ogden. Dougherty was the top vote getter at 2,866, followed by Dunn Lee with 2,280, Sudduth received 1,965, Ogden 1,860 and Townsend

1,218. All three incumbents were, thus, re-elected, though Ogden would win a seat on the Board in several years' time.

Both of the Clerk positions were up for their regular elections in 2010. Incumbent Circuit Clerk Patsy Noland resigned in 2009 to take a seat on the County Commission. Appointed to take over from her was Laura Storm Rattenni, who had worked as a deputy clerk in the office for several years. She opted to run for a full six-year term and faced Republican Edward Compton. Neither Rattenni nor Compton faced a Primary and she was returned to the office for a full six-year term, winning 54% of the vote.

Jennifer Maghan filed for a second term as County Clerk. Her Democratic opponent was Ronda Lehman, a nurse and expert medical witness. Neither had a Primary opponent. Lehman had heavy support from the Democratic Party but came up short. Maghan was re-elected to a second term with 56% of the vote. I think this was one of the last races in which the slow growth community collectively supported a Republican candidate. Maghan had benefited from their support in 2004 and it was repeated six years later. She also had a base of strengthen in the Shepherdstown area, which always turns out at a high rate during most elections.

The Charles Town and Shepherdstown County Commission seats were up in 2010. Both Democratic incumbents filed for second terms. Dale Manuel, the Charles Town member, was unopposed in the Primary and advanced to the General to face Republican Derek Lambert. Much like the race for the 58th District, I don't recall seeing signs for Lambert or witnessing any sort of campaign operation on his part. Manuel had defeated incumbent Republican Commissioner Al Hooper in 2004 and saw his margin decrease just a bit this time, but he still won with 54% of the vote to Lambert's 46%.

The Shepherdstown race was much more entailed. Incumbent Democrat Jim Surkamp drew two Primary challengers, Paul G. Taylor, a Martinsburg criminal defense attorney, and Ruth McQuade, a Shepherdstown area attorney who had previously worked as a federal prosecutor and assistant West Virginia Attorney General. On the issues, McQuade and Surkamp weren't too far apart. I know with both of them running it diluted the slow residential growth and environmental pool of voters and enabled Taylor to slip through to the General Election. He tallied 1,286 votes, followed by Surkamp at 931, and McQuade at 927.

The Republican Party nominated retired businessman Walt Pellish. Dissatisfied with the Democratic nominee, a cadre of more progressive Democrats, Independents, and Republicans who favored controls on residential growth encouraged a movement for an independent candidate. Ed Dunleavy, who had been very active with the Shepherdstown Battlefield Preservation Association decided to run.

I struggled with this race a lot. I had known Surkamp for a number of years and was also quite impressed with McQuade's background and campaign. My position on the rapid nature of residential growth was in line with both of them and I found Taylor to be rather evasive when it came to some of the most important issues. Had McQuade been the nominee, I'm pretty sure she would have beaten Pellish. I think Surkamp, too, would have had a fighting chance, though it is always harder with a voting record. Pellish won with a plurality, receiving 40% to Taylor's 39%. Dunleavy received 21%. I suppose it is possible had Dunleavy not run that Taylor would have won. With Surkamp's loss, the Commission was set to once again have a Republican member, after being totally populated by Democrats for two years.

I think we began to see a shifting of Jefferson County back to purple territory after a couple of banner years. Democrats still fared well, but weren't sure winners, as they had mostly been in the past two cycles.

[1] Carte Patrick Goodwin, Biographical Directory of the United States Congress, Office of the House Historian, Dec. 24, 2019, https://bioguide.congress.gov/search/bio/g000561.

[2] "Perennial Candidate Sheirl Fletcher Files for Senate Run." *Charleston Gazette* Jun 10, 2013.

10

The Special Election of 2011

With the election of Governor Joe Manchin to the United States Senate, a Special Election was necessary to fill the empty Governor's chair. At this point West Virginia didn't have a Lieutenant Governor, as many other states did, and there wasn't a precedent for a Governor leaving office before the completion of his term. Earl Ray Tomblin, who was then the President of the West Virginia Senate eventually became Governor and a special election was called to fill out the remaining term. The Democratic Primary drew six candidates and the Republican Primary eight. The Primary Election was to be held on May 14, 2011, and the General would be on October 4th.

As this was a Special Election in a year in which no other elections were occurring in the state, except for municipal elections, candidates really had nothing to lose by running. They wouldn't need to leave a current office or not run for another term if they happened to be an incumbent. Clearly this was a fairly attractive offer for a number of people.

The Democrats who filed were Acting President of the West Virginia Senate Jeff Kessler, West Virginia Treasurer John Perdue, West Virginia Secretary of State Natalie Tennant, Arne Moltis, Speaker of the West Virginia House Rick Thompson, and Acting Governor Earl Ray Tomblin. We've always been a Tennant family, so I happily supported and donated to Natalie's campaign. I recall speaking with some voters before the Primary who were a bit stumped because they felt as though there were too many good candidates from whom to choose. I know at least three people who felt that way who voted for Acting Governor Tomblin, because he was already in the position.

Interestingly, when the voting occurred Tomblin won basically everywhere unless a candidate had a regional pocket of support. Kessler did well in the Northern Panhandle and Tennant won her base of Monongalia and Marion Counties. Tomblin took 40% of Democratic Primary votes overall. Speaker Thompson was next with 24%, then Tennant at 17%, Perdue at 12.5%, Kessler at 5% and Moltis at about one half of a percent. The Jefferson County results were a little different. Tomblin came in first with 834 votes, followed by Tennant with 413, Kessler at 345, Thompson and Perdue with 284 each, and Moltis at 7.

The Republican field was even more crowded with eight candidates, including State Senator Clark Barnes, State Delegate Mitch Carmichael, former State Delegate Larry Faircloth, former Secretary of State Betty Ireland, Putnam County Prosecuting Attorney Mark Sorsaia, and businessman Bill Maloney. I remember thinking Secretary Ireland would be the winner without trouble and I think a lot of local Republicans thought the same thing. She probably would have been the most formidable Republican to be nominated, but she came in a surprising second. Maloney was first with 45%, then Ireland at 31%, Barnes with 9.5%, Sorsaia at 5%, Faircloth at 4%, Carmichael around 3%, and the rest went to the remaining candidates. Ireland carried Jefferson County, however, with 480 votes, followed by Faircloth at 328, Maloney at 295, and Barnes at 98. The remaining 84 votes were spread out among the other four candidates. Maloney had never served in public office before and if 2010 taught us anything, it was that non-politician politicians were the flavor of the year and it continued into 2011. Had Ireland been nominated, she would have become the first Republican woman to be nominated for Governor and only the second major female gubernatorial candidate in West Virginia's history.

The General Election saw Tomblin and Maloney joined by Bob Henry Baber (Mountain Party), Marla Ingels (Independent), Harry Bertram (American Third Position), and three write-in candidates. Tomblin ran as a conservative Democrat and focused on his record and ability to get things accomplished for West Virginia. Maloney's campaign sort of felt like a "burn it to the ground and start over approach." Baber ran far to the left of Tomblin but didn't draw much support. He did, however, happen to drop into a poetry reading event that the Shepherd University English Honor Society sponsored when I was president, at the Blue Moon Café in Shepherdstown. In a light turn out contest, Tomblin held onto the seat with 149,202 votes to Maloney's 141,656, and Baber's 6,083. Even though Tomblin only served approximately 1 year as Acting Governor, he would only be eligible to serve one additional term if he chose to run again in 2014.

Earl Ray Tomblin was born in Logan County on March 15, 1952, to Earl and Freda Tomblin who owned a restaurant in Chapmanville. His father served as a Justice of the Peace and then as Sheriff of Logan County. Tomblin was first elected to the West Virginia House in 1974, at the age of 22, while still a student at West Virginia University. He served a total of six years before beginning the first of eight terms in the West Virginia Senate. Tomblin rose to be Chairman of the Finance Committee and in 1995 he became the President of the Senate, a position he held twice as long as the previous record holder, a total of 6,150 days. Tomblin holds a bachelor's degree from WVU and a Master's Degree from Marshall University. His wife, Joanne

Tomblin, was named President of Southern West Virginia Community and Technical College in 1999.

11

The Election of 2012

Since 2012 featured a Presidential race, all of the Board of Public Works, and four-year county offices were on the ballot as well. Which meant another busy year, of course.

I think it important to mention at the onset that President Obama remained very unpopular in West Virginia. There have been many reasons thrown around for that, most without any empirical evidence. Suggestions were made that West Virginians were just too ethnically biased to accept an African American president, that the state had just soured on Democrats (especially with the death of Senator Byrd), and some blamed the prevalence of biased and false news reporting services that had become the norm. Perhaps we will never know. I mention this because the incumbent president received an astonishingly small 59% of the vote in the Democratic Primary. The recipient of the other 41% was Keith Judd, a convicted felon. Owing to the unpopularity of President Obama, many Republican candidates attempted to connect any Democrat on the ballot with him, though it didn't have much of an impact at the state level.

As usual the Republican Primary was pretty much settled by the time West Virginia voted. Only five Republicans filed here: Mitt Romney; Rick Santorum; Ron Paul; Newt Gingrich; and Buddy Roemer. Romney took 70% of the vote to Santorum's 12% and Paul's 11%.

Even though Joe Manchin had been elected to the Senate in 2010, the election only covered the last two years of Senator Byrd's term, which meant he had to face voters again in 2012. Once again former Republican West Virginia Delegate Sheirl Fletcher filed in the Democratic Party, following her runs in 2008 and 2010. Manchin was renominated by Democrats 80% to 20% and was set to face 1984, 2006, and 2010 Republican nominee and businessman John Raese. Bob Henry Baber, the former mayor of Richwood, of the Mountain Party was also to appear on the General Election ballot.

One of Raese's more incendiary statements came when he criticized an indoor smoking ban. "But in Monongalia County now, I have to put a huge sticker on my buildings to say this is a smoke-free environment. This is brought to you by the government of Monongalia County. Okay? Remember Hitler used to put [a] Star of David on everybody's lapel, remember that? Same thing."[1]

I recall during the race that Raese's answer to most of the problems facing the United States was to roll back regulations, especially in relation to the environment. He also favored the reduction of taxes. Baber pivoted to the other side, calling for strengthening environmental regulations. Manchin ran as a down the line moderate, as he often did and declared he'd be willing to work with anyone, regardless of political ideology, if it was to the betterment of West Virginia. In the end, the margin wasn't close. Manchin won 52 of the 55 counties and received approximately 61% of the vote to Raese's 36% and Baber's 3%. Raese carried only Grant, Preston, and Doddridge Counties, all typically reliably red areas.

After repeated attempts by the Democratic Party in West Virginia to defeat Shelley Moore Capito in the Second Congressional District, the prospect had begun to fall off the radar. She turned back a spirited challenge in 2010 by Virginia Lynch Graf and 2012 didn't witness a rematch or the attraction of top tier challengers. Interestingly, Capito was challenged by two Republicans in her Primary that year.

Three Democrats filed for the nomination. Howard Swint, who had challenged incumbent Democrat Bob Wise, also in the Second District, in 1996, and ran for the nomination in 2004 as well, filed. Also seeking the nomination were William McCann, a slot machine technician, and IT specialist Dugald Brown, from Berkeley County. From what I can recall about the race, Brown and McCann definitely ran as conservative Democrats in regard to guns. Brown also talked about ensuring the social safety net remained intact. Swint was more progressive, and I remember his suggestion that the deficit be reduced by a reduction in defense spending. He was also a proponent of campaign finance reform. On Primary Day Swint received the most votes, and the nomination, with 48%, followed by McCann at 29%, and Brown at 23%.

On the Republican side, West Virginia House of Delegates member Jonathan Miller, from Berkeley County, and Michael Davis both filed against Capito. Miller opted not to seek a fourth term representing the 53rd District. He largely seemed to suggest that his decision to run was based solely upon religion. He proclaimed that "God is calling me to run for this office now."[2] In a telephone interview with Jenni Vincent of *The Martinsburg Journal*, Miller said "In 2009, I rededicated my life to Christ and began to pray to see even more of God's will for my life. For example, should I stay or leave politics. ... And in May 2010, he called me to run in May 2012."[3] I think it's safe to say Miller ran to the right of Capito. She ended up receiving 83% of the vote to Miller's 11% and Davis's 6%.

I will argue that most of the air was sucked out of the room when it came to the United States Houses races in West Virginia in 2012, owing to the contested races for Senate and Governor. Capito stayed above the fray and, at least from my standpoint, didn't pay much attention to her Democratic opponent. She was easily re-elected to what would be her last term in the United States House by a 70% to 30% margin.

Incumbents Earl Ray Tomblin, Natalie Tennant, Glen Gainer, and John Perdue each sought re-election to their positions as Governor, Secretary of State, Auditor, and Treasurer. Gus Douglass announced his retirement as Commissioner of Agriculture after a record 11 terms. More on that in a minute. Incumbent Attorney General Darrell McGraw was defeated by former New Jersey congressional candidate and Jefferson County resident Patrick Morrisey in a definite surprise.

The race for Governor was something of a repeat from the year before when a Special Election was held to fill out the remainder of Joe Manchin's second term as Governor. Earl Ray Tomblin filed for re-election and even though he'd only served a portion of a term, if he won, this would be considered his second term and he'd be barred from running again. One of the 2010 challengers, Arne Moltis, filed again and took 16% of the vote to Tomblin's 84%.

On the Republican side 2010 nominee and drilling company owner Bill Maloney filed again. The crowded field of 2010 didn't materialize this time and only WVU philosophy professor Ralph William Clark also filed. Much like Tomblin's own Primary victory, Maloney was nominated by a lopsided 84% to 16% margin. Thus, the stage was once again set for a Tomblin vs. Maloney election.

I recalled the extremely negative tone of the 2011 campaign and at least one media outlet suggested it was likely to continue. *The*

Daily Mail reported on Maloney's announcement of candidacy by writing "The race between Democrat Governor Earl Ray Tomblin and Republican challenger Bill Maloney picked up Thursday where it left off last fall: dancing near the gutter."[4] During his announcement Maloney "made unspecified allegations of corruption" against Tomblin.[5] The narrative was quite common with the advent of the Tea Party. Given Tomblin's long history in West Virginia politics, he was first elected to the West Virginia House in 1974 at the age of 22, the allegations were likely to stick easier than if he had no history in elective politics, like Maloney.

Tomblin and Maloney were joined by Mountain Party nominee Jesse Johnson, who had run for Governor and United States Senate in the past, as well as Libertarian David Moran. Johnson, as in past campaigns, made campaign finance reform and the elimination of mountain top removal a high priority. Maloney definitely ran a hard right campaign and Johnson definitely ran a progressive campaign. As in 2011, Tomblin hewed to the middle, declaring himself anti-choice and opposed to most gun restrictions, yet also discussing the importance of education funding and expanding and diversifying West Virginia's economy. 2012 was another close one with Tomblin performing slightly better than in 2011. He received 50% of the vote to 46% for Maloney and 3% for Johnson.

First-term Democratic Secretary of State Natalie Tennant filed for re-election and was unopposed in the Primary. Her Republican opponent, a social studies teacher and first-term West Virginia Delegate, was Brian Savilla from Putnam County. Tennant won easily, tallying 62% of the vote. Interestingly, according to his LinkedIn account, Savilla now lives in Missouri and teaches at Jefferson High School there.

Glen B. Gainer, III, sought what would be his last term as West Virginia Auditor in 2012. He was first elected in 1992 and had little trouble being re-elected every four years. He was the only Democrat who filed and only one Republican filed, West Virginia Delegate and candidate for Governor, Larry V. Faircloth. I will argue Faircloth was Gainer's strongest opponent in any of his races for two reasons. First, as we'll see with some other races in the near future, Faircloth's residency in the Eastern Panhandle enabled him to rack up votes in one of the fastest growing portions of the state. Additionally, he had a history in elective politics and was a veteran campaigner. Still, he only managed 43% to Gainer's 57%, but it was the closest race for Auditor in decades. With his loss, Faircloth was now out of elective office for the first time in almost a quarter of a century, having represented south Berkeley County for 12 terms (24 years) in the West Virginia House of Delegates.

Also running for re-election was West Virginia Treasurer John Perdue, who was first elected in 1996. There was a contested Republican Primary to face him. West Virginia State Senator William Mike Hall defeated Putnam County Assistant Prosecuting Attorney Steve Connolly 56% to 44%. As with Gainer's win, Perdue's margin of victory narrowed from previous years, but he still won 55% of the vote and a fifth term in office.

While the position of Commissioner of Agriculture might be a bit more under the radar than some of the other Board of Public Works offices, it is a very important office for the state, given the wide variety of agricultural pursuits from traditional farming to cottage craft and small plot farming. Incumbent Gus Douglass began his work with the Department in 1957 as an Assistant Commissioner. He was elected to his first term in 1964 and was re-elected in 1968, 1972, 1976, 1980, 1984, 1992, 1996, 2000, 2004, and 2008. In 1988 he sought the office of Governor, finishing fourth in the Democratic Primary. Douglass's 40-plus year tenure made him the longest serving Commissioner of Agriculture in the country.[6]

The race to succeed Douglass was crowded, just as it had been in 1988. Five Democrats filed for the seat, including former WV Delegate Bob Tabb, who had represented the 56th Delegate District in Jefferson County and Sally Shepherd, who had run in 1988, as well. The victor was State Senator Walt Helmick, who captured 33% of the vote. Shepherd was second with 25%, former West Virginia State Senator Steve Miller received 22%, Joe Messino 14% and Tabb 7%. The Eastern Panhandle was firmly in Tabb's corner, and I didn't hear much from the other candidates, except for Helmick who is from Pocahontas County and, thus, not that far away.

Helmick would end up facing farmer and retired Marine Corps Lt Colonel Kent Leonhardt in the General. Leonhardt, who engages in livestock farming, went after Helmick on two fronts. First, he contended that Helmick's long career in elective office was a negative and reflected the much-maligned career-politician profession. Second, he argued that Helmick wasn't a true farmer. Helmick certainly had a rather diversified career, having worked as a teacher, auctioneer, and owned a bottled water company, as well as maintaining 200 acres of farmland.[7] The race was close, but Helmick prevailed with 52% of the vote to Leonhardt's 48%.

The surprise of the night for me was the victory of Morrisey over incumbent West Virginia Attorney General Darrell McGraw. The margin was very close, 51%-49%. The postmortem on the race seemed to be centered around the desire to have a new face in the office. McGraw and his relations had been in elective politics for decades. He is a former Supreme Court Justice (having served from 1976-1988), as is his brother Warren, and had served as Attorney General since 1993. He was re-elected without trouble until 2004, when he received barely 50% of the vote. This repeated itself in 2008. McGraw went on to run for Supreme Court again in 2016, the first year of nonpartisan judicial elections and he came in second to Beth Walker.

I believe Morrisey's victory was an important warning sign that a lot of Democrats didn't heed. It would be only two years later that former Maryland Republican Party Chairman Alex Mooney would succeed Shelley Moore Capito as the Second District Representative after having just moved to the state. On the whole I see nothing wrong with political candidates coming to a state and then seeking office, as long as they have a demonstrable tie to the community and are present and involved. So, while I disagree with Morrisey on nearly every issue, I do appreciate the fact that I've run into him at local events. I can't say the same for all those involved in politics, though. With the increasing population in the Eastern Panhandle, it shouldn't have been a surprise to see someone get a foothold in Republican politics here. I, however, fear that at times we vote based on geography and not upon our best interests.

Two seats on the West Virginia Supreme Court were before voters in 2012. Incumbent Justices Robin Jean Davis and Thomas McHugh occupied those seats. McHugh had served on the Court from 1980 until 1992 and returned to the Court in 2008 when Justice Joseph Albright was on medical leave. Albright ended up dying and Governor Joe Manchin appointed McHugh to the vacant seat. McHugh was forced to run for the remaining two years of the term in 2010, a race he won. During that election he indicated he would not serve beyond 2013.

Davis filed for another term and was joined by attorneys John "Buck" Rogers and Tish Chafin, Wood County Circuit Judge J.D. Beane, Supreme Court clerk Louis Palmer, and Greenbrier County Circuit Judge Jim Rowe. Davis was renominated with 83,071 votes and Chafin received the second slot, garnering 80,393 votes. Rowe, who had also run in 2004, came in third with 59,185 votes and was followed by Bean, then Rogers, and finally Palmer.

On the Republican side two candidates filed and automatically became the nominees. Allen Loughry, who had worked for Congressman Harley O. Staggers, Jr. and Governor Gaston Caperton, and Circuit Judge John Yoder were set to face Davis and Chafin in November. As Yoder was based in the Eastern Panhandle, he did very well here, but came in third overall. Robin Jean Davis was re-elected to another 12-year term with 294,882 votes and Loughry won the second seat, taking 284,299 votes. Yoder received 258,213 and Chafin 248,284 votes. The Court now had two Republicans for the first time since 1977.

Two races were decided in the Primary Election of 2012. Two seats on the Board of Education were filed and one Conservation District Supervisor position was as well. Incumbent CDS G. Warren "Jim" Mickey was re-elected without opposition. Six candidates vied for two seats on the Jefferson County Board of Education. Incumbent Gary Kable filed for re-election and was joined by physical therapist Laurie Ogden, retired teacher and principal Mark Osbourn, retired teacher Jim Jenkins, former Board President Lori Stilley, and Tom Delauney. The second incumbent, Alan Sturm, opted not to seek re-election.

On a personal note, this was an interesting set of candidates for me. Osbourn retired as Principal of C.W. Shipley Elementary School and had been there during my time as a student. Additionally, Jenkins had worked at Shipley and was my sixth-grade teacher. I had known Kable for years and he was the photographer who took my senior pictures. Although Jefferson County continues to grow, one of the virtues of it still being relatively small is the ability to create connections with potential elected officials.

The victors were Osbourn drawing 3,016 votes and Kable 2,323. They were followed by Ogden with 1,935, Jenkins at 1,496, Stilley at 1,246, and Delauney at 738. These two seats remain the most consistent on the Board for their record of re-electing the incumbents, as we'll see in the years to come.

The race for County Commission was a repeat of 2006. Incumbent Democrat Frances Morgan sought re-election and former County Commissioner Jane Tabb filed to reclaim her seat. Tabb faced a primary from Reece Clabaugh, who owned a landscaping business and worked as a real estate agent. Clabaugh benefited from support from the residential development and construction community and ran to the right of Tabb. She prevailed by 9 percentage points.

If 2002 through 2008 was a reaction to unplanned and ex- plosive residential growth in Jefferson County, 2012 continued a trend started in 2010, of the issue quieting down. I suppose part of it was ow- ing to the drop in the housing market, but also the complacency of a constituency once a goal is achieved set in. In 2006 the race between Morgan and Tabb was clearly a proxy war over residential growth in the community. That didn't seem to be as much of an issue in 2012. Tabb reclaimed her seat and defeated Morgan by approximately 16%, making her the only County Commissioner in recent memory to re- turn to the body after an absence.

Senator Herb Snyder filed for another term in the WV Sen- ate. Snyder, a former County Commissioner, served from 1997 until 2005 and again since 2009. He was unopposed in the primary and faced businessman and former County Commissioner Jim Ruland in the general election. Ruland owned commercial property in Bardane that abuts the Burr Industrial Park and had served in the Navy. He was elected to one term on the Jefferson County Commission, from 1997 until 2003, before retiring. I considered Ruland to be a sort of Reagan Republican who talked a lot about low taxes, less regulation, and the need to shrink government. A side note, he, along with Commission- ers Jane Tabb and Al Hooper, supported impact fees when they were first implemented in Jefferson County. Snyder ended up winning by a slightly more comfortable margin than in 2008. He took 54% of the vote to Ruland's 46%.

The House of Delegates races were a bit different this year. Owing to the census and the population growth in Jefferson County, three seats were now allocated to us and new numbers were assigned. The 58th District became the 65th District and covered Ranson, Charles Town, and a few rural areas around the two towns. The 57th District became the 67th and took in Shepherdstown, Harpers Ferry, Bolivar, and part of the Blue Ridge. The 56th District lost the parts of Berkeley County it held and encompassed most of the rural areas in the County, including Kearneysville, Leetown, Kabletown, Rippon, Middleway, Summit Point, and the other half of the Blue Ridge. It was numbered the 66th.

These changes caused a number of moving pieces to come into play. First, incumbent Delegate Eric Householder (56th District) lived in Berkeley County and was drawn into a new District, not covering any of Jefferson County, therefore creating an open seat. Delegate John Doyle (57th District) announced his retirement. Democrat Tiffany Lawrence (58th District), thus became the only incumbent on the ballot in 2012. We'll start there first.

Lawrence was first elected in 2008 and was, at the time, the youngest woman ever elected to the West Virginia Legislature. Considered a fiscal moderate who was more liberal on social issues, her profile fit well with the new 65th District. She faced a political newcomer in Republican Jill Upson. I'm told Upson presented a conservative message with some moderation in 2012 (this would change in 2014). Lawrence ran on her record of securing funds for local schools and libraries and highlighting the legislation she passed. She retained her seat by a close 286 votes out of 6,900 cast.

The open race for the 66th drew one Republican and one Democrat. Paul Espinosa, an employee of Frontier Communications and former president of the Jefferson County Chamber of Commerce, was selected by the Republicans. His father had worked in the horse racing industry, an important constituency in that district. Democrats nominated John Maxey, owner of a data processing firm that was based, at the time, in historic Harpers Ferry. Maxey, a resident of the Blue Ridge, had previously served on the Jefferson County Planning Commission and as President of the Jefferson County Democratic Association. He emphasized the need for representation for the Blue Ridge, as well as environmental and technology issues. I'd say Maxey's campaign was a bit more pragmatic than Espinosa's, which was more down the line, traditional Republican. Espinosa benefited from being well known in the community, as he had resided in Jefferson County his whole life. While Maxey was a native West Virginian, he was born in Boone County and lived in Monongalia County for a number of years. In the end Espinosa won by 20 percent.

The 67th District also featured an open seat owing to Delegate Doyle's retirement. Charles Town attorney Stephen Skinner announced his intention to run. Skinner's father, John, had previously served as Prosecuting Attorney for Jefferson, as had his uncle, Robert. Republicans nominated Elliot Simon, who had run against Doyle the previous cycle. Skinner won and became the first openly LGBTQ legislator in West Virginia. Skinner received 55% of the vote to Simon's 45%.

2012 also saw the re-election of Assessor Angie Banks, Prosecuting Attorney Ralph Lorenzetti, and Sheriff Bobby Shirley, though only Banks was unopposed in the Primary.

Banks faced her 2008 opponent, Gary Dungan, in her quest for a second term. Banks came in first in a tight primary that year to take over from longtime incumbent Ginger Bordier, who was retiring. Dungan, a retired banker, was quite active with the local and state Republican Parties. Banks prevailed by a similar margin as she did in 2008, 11,410 votes to Dungan's 9,628.

Lorenzetti, who was first elected in 2008, faced no Republican opponent that year and wouldn't in 2012 either. However, in both cycles he was opposed by Ruth McQuade, a Shepherdstown area attorney, who had also run for in the primary for the Shepherdstown County Commission seat in 2010. I wasn't actively watching the primary for this race, but from the best I can tell, there wasn't a lot of space between the two of them, with both promising to run an efficient office and strive to save taxpayer dollars. McQuade did talk about being tough on crime in some of her campaign literature and highlighted her time as a federal prosecutor.

The race for Sheriff featured incumbent, Shirley, as well as former two-term Sheriff Ed Boober, who served from 2001 until 2009. Shirley won the Democratic nomination by a vote of 2,224 to 1,127. The General Election was much closer with Republican Earl Ballenger only losing by 399 votes out of 21,000 cast. Part of the reason for the closeness of the race is covered in the next chapter as Shirley ended up in prison and didn't serve out his full second term.

This would be the last election in which Magistrates ran in partisan races. Beginning in 2016, all judicial races were officially nonpartisan. Jefferson County was still allotted three seats and four Democrats ran in the Primary and three Republicans. Incumbents Bill Sensensey, Mary Paul Rissler, and Gail Boober were all renominated with the fourth candidate, Wendy Torelli, coming in last and appearing on the General ballot. The three Republicans all immediately advanced to the General, Ronnie Bell, Peter Onoszko, and Bill Arnicar. Bell ended up dropping out and didn't appear on the General Election ballot. The Democratic incumbents were re-elected with Boober receiving 10,495 votes, Senseney 10,393, and Rissler 10,060. Arnicar was next with 7,631 and Onoszko was fifth with 7,600.

[1] Luke Johnson, "John Raese Equates Smoking Ban to Hitler Policy," *Huffington Post* Apr. 19, 2012.

[2] Jenni Vincent "Miller Announces Congressional Bid." The Martinsburg Journal May 11, 2011.

[3] Jenni Vincent "Miller Announces Congressional Bid." The Martinsburg Journal May 11, 2011.

[4] Ry Rivard and Jared Hunt "Maloney Ready for Another Shot Against Tomblin." Charleston Daily Mail Jan. 26, 12.

[5] Ibid.

[6] "Biography of Gus Douglass," West Virginia Department of Agriculture, https://agriculture.wv.gov/divisions/executive/WVAFHOF/Documents/biosNEW/Douglass,%20Gus.pdf

[7] W.Va. Commissioner of Agriculture candidate: Walt Helmick Herald-Dispatch. Oct. 4, 2016.

12

The Election of 2014

    2014 was an interesting jump back into active work with politics for me. I was elected, unopposed, to the Democratic Executive Committee from the Middleway District, a seat my grandfather, Herbert W. Everhart, held from 1960 until 1964. While I had certainly been paying attention to local races, my interest and focus had been on Congressional races across the country, especially those featuring female and/or ethnic minority candidates. That interest would sync up with state politics as West Virginia was poised to elect its first female United States Senator.

    There weren't too many races on deck this year. The aforementioned United States Senate seat, two County Commission seats, three Board of Education seats, one West Virginia State Senate seat, and an unexpired term for Sheriff. Of course, these races were joined by the always on the ballot United States House seat and three West Virginia House seats.

    Much to my sadness, United States Senator Jay Rockefeller announced he wouldn't seek a sixth term. As I've written earlier, I was lucky enough to work as a summer intern in his Washington, DC office. While this isn't exactly an earth-shattering thing to do, as hundreds and hundreds of interns descend on DC every year, for me it was very special as Rockefeller has long been one of my political heroes and has always been much admired in the family. As a more practical matter, given the fact Senator Byrd had died just four years before, West Virginia was losing clout in Congress at a herculean pace. Two major candidates jumped into the race, along with several lesser-known folks. On the Republican side the only Republican woman to have thus far served in the US House from West Virginia, Shelley Moore Capito announced. Several Democrats considered the race, though in the end West Virginia Secretary of State Natalie Tennant consolidated support. Regardless of the outcome, West Virginia would finally have a female United States Senator.

John Davison Rockefeller, IV, was born on June 18th, 1937, in New York City. After graduating from Harvard, he came to West Virginia as a VISTA volunteer in Emmons, Kanawha County from 1964-66. He told me he immediately fell in love with West Virginia and its people. In 1966 he was elected to the state House of Delegates and served a single term before being elected Secretary of State. In 1972 he launched a bid for governor and won the primary with 73% of the vote, but lost to incumbent Arch Moore, Jr., tallying 350,462 votes to Moore's 423,817. After his loss he became the President of West Virginia Wesleyan College until 1976.[1]

Moore was term limited in 1976 and Rockefeller jumped into the race again, which was more crowded than four years prior. Joining Rockefeller were seven other candidates, including former Congressman Ken Hechler and 1968 nominee James Sprouse. Rockefeller prevailed, receiving 50% of the vote. In the General, he beat former Governor Cecil Underwood by an almost two to one margin. In 1980 he again faced Moore but won 401,863 votes to Moore's 337,240. The stars aligned as US Senator Jennings Randolph opted to retire in 1984, just as Rockefeller was completing his final term in the Governor's

Mansion. The General Election proved to be close as Rockefeller took 52% of the vote to businessman John Raese's 48%. This was the only close race Rockefeller faced for the rest of his career. He was easily re-elected in 1990, 1996, 2002, and 2008.

I was very excited to support and help Secretary Tennant in her bid for the Senate. As expressed before, I've always been in her camp, and I still believe she was the best candidate for our state. In the summer of that year, Massachusetts Senator Elizabeth Warren visited Shepherdstown to endorse Tennant. I acted as a go-between for the campaign and the local Democrats for this event. Fittingly, it was held in the Rockefeller Ballroom of the Clarion Hotel. We easily had 350+ people in attendance, including folks from multiple counties. Senator Warren gave a wonderful speech and was warmly received. I recall seeing individuals in attendance who typically don't turn out for local political events.

We later held a get out the vote rally with Tennant and former Congressman Harley O. Staggers, Jr. Staggers represented the Eastern Panhandle in the House for a decade before the 1990 Census caused us to lose a seat. His home of Keyser was redrawn into the First District, and we were drawn into Congressman Bob Wise's District. The former Congressman, his brother Danny, and son Bryan attended and presented our inaugural Congressman Harley O. Staggers, Sr., Award to former Jefferson County Democratic Party Vice-Chairwoman Kay Bresee, owing to her decades of service to the local Party. This was the first time I met the Staggers brothers, although I knew Bryan from Shepherd.

The Staggers family has been very kind to the Jefferson County Democrats over the years, always attending our Byrd Dinner and presenting the Staggers Award. Their continued commitment to West Virginia and the Democratic Party is appreciated by many. I find too often when an elected official retires from office that he or she often stops lending support to the Party, which is unfortunate. This can't be said of the Staggers Family.

While Tennant barnstormed the state and had won more votes than Capito in their respective Primaries, the unpopularity of the Obama White House and the changing tides of West Virginia politics proved to be too much. Capito prevailed and Republicans regained control of the United States Senate. I look at her loss not as a repudiation of Tennant herself, or her work as Secretary of State, but rather as the emerging difficulty of winning statewide as a Democrat in West Virginia—a trend that was only going to worsen with the dawn of the Trump Age.

I do want to zero in on the odd footing of this race. Tennant had been elected statewide twice by this point, had the support of the unions populated by the miners, teachers, and other forces in the labor movement, and was running in a state with more registered Democrats than Republicans, yet she still lost. I think a small part of this is attributed to residual fondness of Capito's father, Governor Moore. (We know West Virginians love dynastic politics.) Also, as mentioned the unpopularity of President Obama played a part, but there was definitely something else. 2014 was the first year in which I really began to notice that our state's willingness to ticket split, as it had over the past decade and a half, was coming to an end. No longer were voters open to supporting the Republican running for President, yet hand state-based power continually to the Democrats. Further evidence is found in another race that year.

Natalie E. Tennant was born in Fairview, West Virginia, the youngest of seven children. In 1990, while a junior at West Virginia University, she became the first female Mountaineer mascot in the University's history. She received a B.S. Degree in Journalism in 1991 and also took a M.A. Degree in 2002 from WVU. Prior to her service as Secretary of State, she worked as a television journalist and was co-owner of Wells Media Group.[2]

Capito's decision to run for the Senate left her seat in the US House open. Two Democrats filed, former State Democratic Party Chairman Nick Casey and Delegate Meshea Poore. Casey ran as a moderate (or even conservative) Democrat, both in the Primary and General. I supported Poore in the Primary owing to her legislative record and her, what I thought were, superior campaign skills. Had she been elected, Poore would have been the first African American member of Congress to represent West Virginia. On Primary Day Casey won by about two to one.

There was some space between the candidates on the issues. Casey was opposed to abortion rights and indicated he would not support Nancy Pelosi for Speaker of the House, if Democrats regained control of that chamber. We certainly have some Democrats throughout the state who begin to get nervous when a candidate leads with social issues. There were similarities as well, as both candidates had a history of service within the Party and state, and both worked as attorneys.

While he hadn't been my pick in the Primary, I found Casey to be very genuine and earnest in his quest to represent us. It was a pleasure to support him in the General and I appreciated his willingness to campaign in the Panhandle and pay attention to this part of the state. Additionally, he has stayed involved in the Democratic Party since that year's election.

The Republican side was much stranger. Seven candidates filed to run and the surprise winner was former Maryland Republican Party Chairman Alex X. Mooney, who had just recently moved to Charles Town. Mooney received 36% of the vote to Berkeley Springs pharmacist Ken Reed's 22% and 18% for former WV Delegate and International Trade Commission Member Charlotte Lane. It's interesting to note that 58% of the vote went to Eastern Panhandle candidates. I had assumed Lane would be the nominee and hadn't expected Reed to perform as well as he did.

Many local pundits believed Casey would now run away with the race, given his long record of service to West Virginia and Mooney's seeming move to the state perpetrated only to seek federal office. I personally questioned some of the campaign tactics put into place by Casey's staff, though, which seemed to rest heavily on calling voters and not necessarily direct contact with the candidate himself. In something of a surprise, Mooney won with a plurality of the vote, receiving 47%. Casey took 44% and the other 9% was split between Libertarian Davy Jones and Independent Ed Rabel. Rabel, whose background is in journalism, ran to the left of Casey. It isn't hard to imagine many of his supporters considering Casey as a second choice. I could write a whole book about the arguments for and against casting a protest vote for a candidate less in the middle.

I do want to take a moment to address something that I believe some candidates do too often in West Virginia, especially in the Panhandle. As we are one of the few places in the state to be gaining population, it doesn't make much sense, in my mind, to throw around terms like "real West Virginian" when facing a candidate who is newer to the area or who has roots here but hasn't spent his or her whole life in the state. I think it is counterproductive, as it also implies recently arrived West Virginians aren't welcome. I don't think Casey meant to imply this, but it did seem as much from some of his campaign staff.

While I haven't been discussing the other Congressional District races in WV that often, I do want to make a quick mention of the other two, as this year was oddly unsettled. Incumbent Auditor Glen B. Gainer, III, was unopposed for the First District Democratic nomination and was considered to be a top recruit, given his long record of winning statewide races. He faced off against incumbent David

McKinley, who was first elected in 2010. Gainer ended up losing, taking only 36% of the vote. In the Third District, incumbent Nick Joe Rahall, who was first elected in 1976, was challenged in the primary by veteran Richard Ojeda. Former Democratic WV State Senator Evan Jenkins filed as a Republican. Rahall won the primary 66% to 34%, but lost to Jenkins, taking 45% of the vote. For the first time in almost a century, Republicans now controlled a majority of the federal offices in West Virginia.

Kabletown County Commissioner Patsy Noland drew a winning card by not facing any opposition in the Primary or General Election. This was the first time since 1992 that a County Commission seat went uncontested by one of the two parties. As usual, I can't attest to the thinking of the Republican Party or potential candidates, but I believe they understood Noland had strong support from across the political spectrum and that unseating her would be very difficult. Additionally, fewer candidates are running for office in the past decade or so, as our local politics have become just as divisive as those at the national level.

The Harpers Ferry seat was certainly more interesting. Incumbent Democrat Lyn Widmyer announced she wasn't seeking a second term. Democrats nominated Ronda Lehman, who had run for County Clerk in 2010. Republicans picked between Peter Onoszko and Eric Bell. Onoszko ran for Magistrate in 2012. He retired from the Army as a Lt. Colonel. Bell was a total newcomer to politics and, in fact, civic organizations. A Navy veteran, he worked as the operations manager for the Bloomery Distillery.

From my position I thought Onoszko would be the easy victor, as voters were familiar with him and he ran a full campaign of participating in candidate events, appearing at various organizational meetings, and so forth. He was also fairly specific on the issues, hammering property rights and cutting the budget. Bell, however, was much more low key and seemed to be out of his depth when it came to specific policy issues facing the county. He did contend the county's IT systems were out of date and was opposed to the emergency services fee. That being said, he beat Onoszko by 26 votes and was the Republican nominee.

I must admit that I am not a fan of politics on social media, so I'm not always the most aware about what is happening regarding county affairs as viewed through Facebook or Twitter. As I understand it, though, the Republican Party and offshoot organizations like the Liberty PAC, heavily worked Facebook to paint Lehman as an out of touch liberal, though I believe she had a much broader knowledge of county government than Bell. 2014 turned out to be a year in which most seasoned political observers made the wrong predictions. Lehman was thought to be the runaway leader in the race, but she ended up falling short. Bell won by 1,281 votes and became the first openly LGBTQ County Commissioner and the youngest at the time. His service on the Commission would be short lived, however, as will be discussed in the next chapter.

The races for County Commission saw a definite shift in 2014, which has continued largely unbated. In years prior, voters seemed to weight how involved candidates happened to be in civic organizations, their visibility in the community, and their actual ideas and qualifications for the job. Bell's victory over Lehman demonstrates that a majority of voters that year were more interested in voting against the "D" after her name and didn't care about much else. We'll see more of that in the years to come.

The race for Sheriff was a special case. Incumbent Pete Dougherty had been appointed by the County Commission following the resignation of Bobby Shirley. On January 14th of 2013, Shirley pleaded guilty to a federal civil rights violation stemming from his beating of a bank robbery suspect following a high-speed chase. Rather than stand trial he took a plea deal which involved him resigning from the office of Sheriff. He faced up to a 10-year federal prison sentence.[3] Shirley ended up serving only one year.[4] Dougherty had previously served as a probation officer and Magistrate in the County, after which he served on the Board of Education and worked for the Veterans Affairs Department in Washington. If elected, he would only be eligible to serve one more term, as state code limits individuals to two consecutive terms, even if they are only partial.

Dougherty had not been the only applicant for the position. Sixteen individuals applied and the County Commission narrowed the choices to Dougherty, retired Charles Town Chief of Police Louis Brunswick, who had run for the position in 2008, and Steve Groh, an assistant prosecuting attorney. Among the initial pool of applicants were two candidates who faced Shirley in 2012. Former Sheriff Ed Boober had challenged Shirley in the Democratic Primary but came up short. The Republican nominee, Earl Ballenger a retired Jefferson County Deputy, lost the General Election to Shirley. Also applying were retired lieutenant with the Fairfax City Police Walter Smallwood; Kenneth Mills, a bailiff and retired lieutenant from the Sheriff's Department; Ronnie Fletcher, a sergeant with the Sheriff's Department; Gerald Koogle, who had was the Republican nominee in 2008; and retired Montgomery County police officer Willard Liston. Not all applicants had a law enforcement background and those included David Tabb, Francis Casto, Clifford Taylor, Karen Starr Manuel-Gregoryk, Mimi Rogers, and Amanda Piatt.[5]

When it came time for the County Commission to make its decision, Brunswick received two votes, those of Commissioners Lyn Widmyer and Jane Tabb, while Dougherty received the votes of Commissioners Dale Manuel, Patsy Noland, and Walt Pellish. Thus, Dougherty became Sheriff in 2013.

Republicans nominated Steve Sowers and Dougherty was unopposed in the Democratic Primary. I don't remember this being a particularly highly watched race that year. Interestingly, it wasn't uncommon to find Dougherty's signs in a yard with those for all Republican candidates. I believe this demonstrates the broad appeal he enjoyed, and the trust voters placed in him as an honest and forthright public servant.

State Senator John Unger was seeking a fifth term and faced former Delegate Larry Faircloth in November. Faircloth ran with a concentrated focus on jobs, a word that appeared on his signage. The first time I met Faircloth was in 2016 when his wife, Laura, was running for Circuit Judge. My interactions with him are typically only at Democratic functions, which he typically attends with her, just as she attends Republican functions with him. Even though I'm sure we disagree on most political issues, it's easy to see how he has been successful in politics, as he is warm, friendly, and willing to leave a discussion on an upbeat note even if it ends in disagreement. He proved to be quite a strong candidate, though Unger prevailed with 52.5% of the vote and was returned to Charleston.

Jefferson County's three Delegates, Tiffany Lawrence (65th), Paul Espinosa (66th), and Stephen Skinner (67th) all announced their plans to run again. Lawrence would face off against her 2012 opponent, Jill Upson. Espinosa drew no Democratic challenger, but Mountain Party candidate Danny Lutz did run. Patricia Rucker filed to take on Skinner and defeated W. Matthew Harris, 2-to-1 in the Republican Primary.

As mentioned previously, the 65th District takes in Charles Town and Ranson, with some rural areas on the outskirts to the two towns. The voter registration tallies are approximately one third across the board (33% Democrats, 33% Independents, and 33% Republicans). Lawrence was first elected in 2008 and held her seat against a tough campaign by the local and state Republicans in 2012. She was again a top target and fell short this time, taking 1,848 votes to Upson's 2,335. Upson ran as a down the line conservative and 2014 was a year in which more Republicans and conservative Independents turned out than Democrats and liberal Independents. Upson's victory made her the first African American Republican woman to be elected (not to serve) in the WV House and the first African American female legislator from the Eastern Panhandle. Additionally, this was the first legislative race in Jefferson County in which a female legislator was elected to replace another female legislator. Again, there is a caveat. In 1976 Carolyn Snyder was elected to the WV House from Jefferson and when she resigned, she was replaced by Bianca James, who was appointed to the vacancy. James was defeated when she sought the seat in 1978. If you haven't been able to tell by now, I love these obscure political trivia facts!

The 66th District covers much of the rural area in Jefferson County, stretching from Kearneysville to Kabletown and part of the Blue Ridge. Espinosa had been elected to his first term in 2012. While he is certainly a conservative, he seems to hit the economic issues more in his talking points than social issues. The District is overwhelmingly Republican and, I'm sorry to say, the Democratic Party didn't field a challenger that year. However, Danny Lutz ran as a Mountain Party candidate. Lutz is a former Democrat, who had applied for the seat when it was numbered the 56th and was vacant owing to the resignation of Delegate Bob Tabb in 2009. He had also run for the State Senate in the 1980s. Many Democrats in the District supported Lutz, though Espinosa's margin of victory went up from 2012. Espinosa received 3,074 votes to 876 for Lutz.

While Shepherdstown can sometimes take an outsized role in voting in the 67th District, owing to usually high turnout, the District stretches to Harpers Ferry and covers the other half of the Blue Ridge. Skinner was seeking his second term and opinions suggested he'd have a clear path to victory. Rucker, who has a degree in history, ran as a far right conservative and talked about her work with the various conservative groups in Jefferson County and West Virginia. A homeschooler, she focused a lot on social issues. From what I've been told she was a vigorous door to door campaigner. On Election Night she came within 133 votes out of over 5,000 cast of unseating Skinner.

2014 was a good year for Republicans. As I've mentioned, they took a majority of the Congressional races and took both houses of the WV Legislature for the first time in decades. The loss of the 65th District race now meant Stephen Skinner was the only Democrat in the WV House from the Eastern Panhandle. Additionally, Republicans gained a majority on the County Commission with three Republicans (Commissioners Tabb, Pellish, and Bell) and two Democrats (Commissioners Noland and Manuel).

Three seats on the Board of Education were open and decided in the Primary Election. Incumbents Scott Sudduth and Mariland Dunn Lee filed to run again. Larry Togans, a former Board of Education member, had been appointed to fill out the remaining time on Pete Dougherty's term, as Dougherty had been appointed to the vacant Sheriff's position. Togans did not file for a full term. Sudduth and Dunn Lee were joined by accountant Kathy Skinner, teacher Theresa Rinehart, former Board member Alan Sturm, and physical therapist Laurie Ogden. This particular batch of seats seemed to have a fairly high turnover rate from time to time and 2014 was no different.

As I've mentioned before local political watchers often say that serving on the Board is a thankless job and every decision made often angers 50% of the voting population. Skinner came in first, followed by Ogden, and then Sudduth. Dunn Lee lost her seat by about 450 votes. Sturm was next and then Rinehart who had publicly declared that she was withdrawing from contention. With Togan's retirement the Board once again had no African American members, though the number of women did increase by one.

[1] "John Davison Rockefeller, IV," Biographical Directory of the United States Congress, Office of the House Historian, Dec. 24, 2019, https://bioguide.congress.gov/search/bio/R000361.

[2] "Natalie Tennant," *The West Virginia Encyclopedia*, WV Humanities Council, Nov. 21, 2016, http://www.wvencyclopedia.org/articles/2327

[3] Richard F. Belisle, "Three to be Interviewed for Jefferson County Sheriff Position," *Herald-Mail* (Hagerstown, MD) Feb. 27, 2013.

[4] Vicki Smith, "Ex-Jefferson County Sheriff Sentenced to 1 Year in Federal Prison in Beating of Robbery Suspect," *Herald-Mail* (Hagerstown, MD) May 13, 2013.

[5] Richard F. Belisle, "Three to be Interviewed for Jefferson County Sheriff Position," *Herald-Mail* (Hagerstown, MD) Feb. 27, 2013.

13

The Election of 2016

Depending upon to which political party one subscribes, 2016 was either a huge victory or a soul-crushing defeat. Either way it certainly defied what many of us thought we knew about politics.

For those who didn't skip the chapter about 2008, it should come as no surprise that I was a fervent and early supporter of Hillary Rodham Clinton. While she won West Virginia convincingly that year, history didn't repeat itself. Bernie Sanders won our May Primary with 51% to Clinton's 36%. The Republican race was pretty much settled by this time and Donald Trump took 77% of the vote to 9% for Ted Cruz and 7% for John Kasich.

I'll readily admit that Donald Trump's nationwide victory in the Electoral College caught me by surprise. At the start of the cycle, I really thought Secretary Clinton had a chance in West Virginia. I was totally wrong. Ticket splitting was still happening in our state, as some Democrats managed to win even as Clinton received only 26% in our state, the smallest vote share ever for a Democrat here.

While there wasn't a United States Senate seat up in 2016, the always present United States House of Representatives seat did see a crowded Democratic field. Incumbent Republican Alex Mooney, who had won only two years prior, filed for re-election and defeated businessman Marc Savitt 73% to 27% in the Primary. I was surprised a non-Eastern Panhandle based Republican didn't challenge Mooney and hasn't since his initial win.

The Democratic field numbered five with former WV Delegate Mark Hunt, veteran Cory Simpson, veteran and attorney Tom Payne, attorney Harvey Peyton, and frequent candidate Robin Wilson, Jr. Many political observers saw Mooney's victory in 2014 to be a fluke and believed that a strong Democrat had the ability to defeat him. A number of Eastern Panhandle Democrats backed Simpson, given his roots in Kanawha County and his profile as a combat veteran. Peyton had the advantage of being from Putnam County, while both Simpson and Hunt were from Charleston. Payne's address was listed as Berkeley County and his sister had taught in the area for some time, thus giving him a connection to the voting bloc over here, if only based upon his residence.

I had the opportunity to take both Peyton and Simpson around to meet various active Democrats and enjoyed getting to know them both. I think either would have been fine nominees and members of the United States House. Simpson seemed the most likely to gain support from national interest groups, if nominated. The Jefferson County Democratic Association hosted a forum, moderated by Reva Mickey, and invited all five candidates to participate. We were honored to welcome four, with only Wilson not attending. Interestingly Payne, though he spent next to no money and didn't run any ads, won the Panhandle based, I believe, solely upon his address. District wide Hunt came in first with 29%, followed by Simpson at 26%, Payne at 21%, Peyton with 15%, and Wilson rounding it out at 9%.

With a nominee chosen, the Party worked to support Mark Hunt. I found him to be quite personable in one-on-one settings but didn't think he was the best retail campaigner. He did visit the Panhandle on several occasions, and he worked to establish connections here. The Mountain Party opted not to run a candidate in 2016 and endorsed Hunt. In the end it was for naught. Mooney won re-election with 58% of the vote.

All of the Board of Public Works offices were up in 2016. Governor Earl Ray Tomblin was term limited, but incumbents Natalie Tennant, John Perdue, Walt Helmick, and Patrick Morrisey filed for re-election. Long time state Auditor Glen B. Gainer, III had resigned before his term ended and Lisa Hopkins, who was appointed to take over from him, didn't seek the office. Democrats had a Primary battle for several of the races, while Republicans only had one contested Primary.

The race for Governor drew three candidates: Jim Justice; Booth Goodwin; and Jeff Kessler. Justice, the richest person in West Virginia, owned a myriad of businesses, including coal mines, farms, and the Greenbriar Resort. He was also a former Republican. Several longtime Democratic operatives signed up to work on his campaign and he was supported by the Manchin machine. I met him for the first time at a meet and greet at Harewood, here in Jefferson County, and found him to be perfectly personable and approachable. He seemed to focus heavily on the idea that with his wealth he couldn't be bought, and his only aim was to help his birth state.

Booth Goodwin was an US Attorney during the Obama years and was responsible for prosecuting Don Blankenship after a deadly disaster at one of his mines. His father serves as a federal judge and his mother was the longtime West Virginia Secretary of the Arts and Humanities. His cousin, Carte, had been tapped to fill Senator Byrd's seat until the Special Election was held. I met Booth during the campaign and thought he had a very compelling case and background story. He has remained involved and has spoken on legal matters before the Jefferson County Democrats on some panels we've hosted.

The third candidate, Jeff Kessler, was the former West Virginia Lt. Governor and Senate President. He represented the Second Senate District from 1997 until 2017 and had previously run in the special election that Tomblin won when Joe Manchin resigned to become our second United States Senator. He also served as Senate Minority Leader after the Democrats lost their majority.

I like to think the factions within the Democratic Party lined up fairly neatly with the three candidates. Justice attracted the moderate and conservative Democrats, Goodwin had the traditional liberals, and Kessler the progressives. The breakdown wasn't entirely absolute and, in some instances, didn't make a lot of sense. Kessler had an anti-choice voting record and was opposed to some gun regulations, which made it interesting when a lot of Sanders supporters favored him over Goodwin. At the time I argued that West Virginia would have been well served by any of the three candidates occupying the Governor's Mansion. More to come on that later.

Jim Justice managed to win a majority of the Democratic Primary vote with 51%. Goodwin was next with 25% and then Kessler at 23%. The geographic spread was fairly stark. Goodwin, who is from Charleston, won Kanawha and Jackson Counties. Kessler represented Wheeling in the Senate and won four Counties: Wetzel, Marshall, Ohio, and Brooke. Justice won all the remaining 49 counties.

The only Republican who filed was Bill Cole, the President of the West Virginia Senate. He had been appointed to the West Virginia House of Delegates for an unexpired term in 2010 and served until the end of the year. He then defeated Democratic Senator Mark Wills in 2012 to represent the Sixth Senate District, which included all of Mercer County and portions of McDowell, Mingo, and Wayne Counties. Rather than run for a second term, he opted to seek the governorship.

Joining Justice and Cole on the General Election ballot were three third party candidates. The Constitution Party nominated frequent candidate Phil Hudok. David Moran ran as the Libertarian nominee. Charlotte Pritt, a former member of the WV Senate and WV House of Delegates and the 1996 Democratic nominee for Governor, ran as the Mountain Party nominee. There was definitely not a united Democratic Party in 2016. I spoke with several Democrats who believed Justice was too conservative and not strong enough on environmental issues, which caused them to support Pritt. During Justice's speech at the West Virginia Democratic Party Convention, a few dozen delegates left the hall. I believe had Goodwin or Kessler been the nominee, Pritt would not have garnered the support she did.

On Election Day Justice ended up winning with a plurality of the vote, 49%. Cole won 42% and Pritt 6%. Cole won 18 counties, including the entire Eastern Panhandle, while Justice won nearly every southern and central county, as well as most of the Northern Panhandle. He continued the Democratic hold on the seat which was continuous since 2000. Justice's membership in the Democratic Party, though, would be short lived as within a year he switched to the Republican Party at a rally with President Trump.

Incumbent Democratic Secretary of State Natalie Tennant filed for a third term. She faced an opponent in the Democratic Primary for the first time since 2008, WV Delegate Patsy Trecost of Clarksburg, who was finishing his first term in the WV House. His motivation for running was a little unclear, as he didn't seem to have many complaints about the job Tennant was doing. She won the Primary with 77% of the vote and was set to face Mac Warner, who defeated Barry Holstein 63% to 37% in the Republican Primary.

The resulting General Election was very close. Warner, whose brother, Kris, had been the Republican nominee for Governor in 2004, argued Tennant was out of step with West Virginians because she attended the Democratic National Convention as a Delegate for Secretary Clinton. Tennant focused on her modernization of the office and legislative achievements in expanding access to the ballot box for military members. In the end Tennant was defeated by approximately 12,000 votes out of almost 700,000 cast. Warner received 49% of the vote to Tennant's 47%. The remaining 4% was won by Libertarian attorney John S. Buckley.

On a side note, I must say I took Natalie's loss quite hard, topped only by Hillary Clinton's defeat. I can think of few people who have given West Virginian more and who advocate for our state to a greater degree.

For the first time since 1956 there wasn't a candidate named Gainer on the ballot for West Virginia Auditor. Glen B. Gainer, III was first elected in 1992, thereby succeeding his father, Glen B. Gainer, Jr. He was often unopposed and never won by less than 57%. As I covered in a previous chapter, he sought a seat in the United States House in 2014 but was defeated by incumbent David McKinley. Gainer announced in April that he would be resigning early to take a position as CEO of the National White Collar Crime Center.[1] Gainer had already announced he wouldn't be running for another term, so three Democrats and one Republican filed as candidates.

The sole Republican was West Virginia Delegate J.B. McCuskey, who represented the 35th District, based in Kanawha County, from 2013 through 2017. His father, John McCuskey, had served, by appointment, for one year on the West Virginia Supreme Court, 1998. Mary Ann Claytor, Robin Righter, and Jason Pizatella all vied for the Democratic nomination with Gainer's endorsement going to Pizatella.

Jefferson County sought to host a forum for the three Democrats. Claytor accepted the invitation, as did Pizatella. We received
no response from Righter. Unfortunately, a few days before the event
Pizatella cancelled and sent a surrogate to read a prepared statement.
Given her experience and tireless campaigning, after the event I opted
to endorse and strongly support Mary Ann. She campaigned exten-
sively throughout the state and didn't ignore the Eastern Panhandle.

Claytor and Righter had both worked for the West Virginia
Auditor's Office in the past. Pizatella was in Governor Tomblin's cabinet, but had no previous experience with the workings of the office he
sought, nor did McCuskey. A lot of the establishment Democrats lined
up behind Pizatella, presumably given his service to Tomblin. On Primary Day Claytor received 44% of the vote, with Pizatella at 34%, and
Righter at 22%.

Like with many statewide offices, there was a third-party
candidate on the ballot, Brenton Ricketts, who lived in the Eastern Panhandle, which enabled him to run up a larger than usual vote total
in the eastern counties. Claytor hammered McCuskey on his lack of
experience in audits and the basic work of the office. She was out-
spent, though, and McCuskey offered somewhat vague good government promises without talking about his concrete plans for the office.
For the first time in well over half a century, a Republican was elected
WV Auditor. McCuskey took 58% of the vote to Claytor's 35%, with
Ricketts netting 7%.

Incumbent Commissioner of Agriculture Walt Helmick filed
for a second term. He took over from longtime Commissioner Gus
Douglass in 2012. 2016 would be a repeat of the previous election,
as Helmick again faced Kent Leonhardt, who had been elected as a
WV State Senator in 2014. They were joined by Libertarian Buddy
Guthrie. The main components of the race were very much the same
as 2012. Leonhardt played up his status as a veteran and argued

Helmick wasn't a real farmer. This year Leonhardt prevailed with a plurality, 48% to Helmick's 41%. Guthrie received a surprisingly high 10% of the vote. Leonhardt became the first Republican Commissioner of Agriculture since 1992, Cleve Benedict's final year in office.

The lone Republican member of the Board of Public Works, Attorney General Patrick Morrisey, decided to run for a second term and was challenged by West Virginia State Delegate Doug Reynolds, who owned a construction company and several newspapers. Each faced no opposition in their Primaries, but two additional candidates joined them in the General Election. The Libertarian Party nominated Karl Kolenich and Michael Sharley ran as a Mountain Party candidate.

I met Reynolds for the first time at a fundraiser held for him in Charles Town. I found him to be very personable and down to Earth, not to mention he has excellent taste in blazers! He was first elected to the West Virginia House in 2006 and served continuously until 2017. I repeatedly heard the narrative that Reynolds had significant personal funds, which enabled him to self-fund his campaign. I'm not opposed to candidates who self-fund, but I wonder how prudent it was for the Democratic Party to continually mention this, as it may have made some voters feel as though he was out of touch with their daily lives. I want to stress I don't think he was, but perceptions can mean a lot in politics. Reynolds continually hit Morrisey on his closeness to the pharmaceutical industry and the lack of consumer protections offered by his office. Morrisey appealed to Trump voters and ran as an open conservative. I really liked Reynolds and was sorry he didn't win. Morrisey was re-elected with 52% of the vote to 42% for Reynolds, while both third-party candidates received 3% each.

Incumbent Democratic State Treasurer John Perdue opted to seek another term. He was first elected in 1996 and had little trouble being re-elected every four years. 2016 brought two potential Republican challengers, Ann Urling and Larry W. Faircloth. Urling, at the time she filed, was a Senior Vice-President with Summit Community Bank. Faircloth had been first elected to the WV House in 2012 and represented the 60th District. He was re-elected in 2014. His father, Larry V. Faircloth, was a former Delegate. Urling was nominated, tallying 55% of the vote to Faircloth's 45%.

In comparison to the other statewide races, I felt this one flew under the radar. In the entire Eastern Panhandle, I think I saw one yard sign for Urling. A Libertarian was also in the running, Michael Allen Young. There didn't seem to be much doubt that Perdue would win, but the race was closer than I expected. He won with 50%, his lowest percentage ever. Urling took 44% and Young 6%. In the end Perdue would be the only Democratic statewide incumbent who was re-elected, a worrying sign for 2020.

2016 was the first year in which judicial officials were elected in non-partisan elections, meaning all five of our Circuit Judges, our three Family Court Judges, and our three magistrates would only be found on the primary ballot. Longtime Circuit Judge David H. Sanders, first elected in 1992, announced his retirement. There was also a new seat added, bringing the total number of judges to six. Incumbents John Yoder, Christopher C. Wilkes, Gray Silver, III, and Michael D. Lorensen all filed to retain their seats. Judge Sanders's old seat, Division 1, saw three candidates jump in, Berkeley County attorneys Steven Redding and Bridget Cohee, as well as Jefferson County attorney Stephen Kershner. Seeking the new Division 6 seat were former Jefferson County Prosecuting Attorney Ralph Lorenzetti and Berkeley County attorneys Laura V. Faircloth, Bill Powell, and Nick Colvin (who moonlights as a professional wrestler).

Since Judge Gina Groh was confirmed to a federal judgeship, no women held Circuit Judge seats in our Circuit (Jefferson, Berkeley, and Morgan Counties), which was remedied once the votes were counted. Cohee finished first in Jefferson County and also in total when the votes of all three counties were tallied. While Lorenzetti won Jefferson County, Faircloth was the victor when results from the other counties were counted.

So, the line-up was now four male Circuit Judges (Yoder, Wilkes, Silver, and Lorensen) and two female Circuit Judges (Cohee and Faircloth), an all-time high.

The Family Court seats brought less attention. Incumbents David Camilletti (Division 1), Sally Gavin Jackson (Division 2), and David Greenberg (Division 3) all filed for another term. Jackson drew two opponents, both Berkeley County attorneys, Christine L. Glover, who also worked as a public-school teacher, and Tia Coode, but prevailed in both Jefferson County and in total when the votes from Berkeley County were added.

For the first time Jefferson County Magistrate seats weren't filed by the top vote getters, as had been the custom since 1976. Starting in 2016, each seat would be assigned a division and candidates were to pick which division in which to run. Additionally, the positions were now non-partisan. Long time Magistrates Gail C. Boober, Bill Senseney, and Mary Paul Rissler each filed for re-election and picked Divisions 1, 2, and 3 respectively. Each drew one challenger, but all were re-elected. Boober faced Ginny Harrison and won 58% to 42%. Senseney's opponent was attorney Ron Rossi, who received 30% to the incumbent's 70%. In Division 3 Rissler tallied 71% to bailiff Arthur "Skip" Cridler's 29%.

One of the state's five Supreme Court seats was on deck in 2016. Incumbent Brent Benjamin filed for re-election and was joined by attorney and 2008 candidate Beth Walker, former Supreme Court Justice and Attorney General Darrell McGraw, former State Senator Bill Wooton, and attorney Wayne King. As with other judicial offices, this was the first time a Supreme Court race would be decided in a non-partisan primary.

Walker was thought to be the most conservative and pro-business of the candidates, even though Benjamin had been elected as a Republican. Wooton started early and given his history in elected office, began to solidify support among Democrats, which was complicated by McGraw's last-minute entry into the race. As I've written prior, the McGraw family has a very long and fairly successful history in West Virginia politics. Had Wooton and McGraw not both run, it is reasonable to conclude that the one who did would have won the seat. However, that wasn't the case and Walker was elected with 40% of the vote, followed by McGraw at 23%, Wooton at 21%, Benjamin with 12%, and King at 4%. With Walker's election the Supreme Court was majority female for the first time in the state's history, as she joined Justices Margaret Workman and Robin Jean Davis.

Also on the non-partisan docket were two Board of Education seats and two Conservation District Supervisor (CDS) positions. Normally only one CDS is up each cycle, but the resignation of Bobby Gruber left an unexpired term, as well as the open seat, also left open by the retirement of G. Warren "Jim" Mickey. Daniel P. "Danny" Lutz, Jr., filed for the full term and was elected without opposition. A former Democrat, Lutz had vied for the West Virginia State Senate in the 1980s but left the party in recent years and ran as the Mountain Party nominee for the West Virginia House from District 66 in 2014. His sister Nancy Lutz, a retired police officer, filed for the two-year term and faced Richard F. Blue who operates his family's farm near Zoar. Lutz received 4,888 votes to Blue's 4,512, making her the first, and to date, only female Conservation District Supervisor for Jefferson County.

The race for the Board of Education was slightly quieter than the previous cycle. Incumbents Gary Kable and Mark Osbourn both filed for re-election. They were joined by Erica Logan, Ronald L. Jones, and Rob Frazier. Logan, a manager for IBM, and Frazier both had children in or recently in the County school system. Jones, a graduate of Jefferson County schools, works both as an educational consultation and photographer. Kable, a former Jefferson County Commissioner, was first elected to the Board of Education in 2004. Osbourn, the longtime principal of C.W. Shipley Elementary School (and my old principal!) was vying for his second term. On Primary night Osbourn and Kable were both returned, with Logan running a close third.

A slew of local offices was before voters in 2016. Two County Commission seats, Circuit Clerk, County Clerk, Assessor, Sheriff, Prosecuting Attorney, and Surveyor. Both Jennifer Maghan, the County Clerk, and Ralph Lorenzetti, the Prosecuting Attorney, announced they were retiring. This left Circuit Clerk Laura Storm, Assessor Angie Banks, Sheriff Pete Dougherty, and Commissioners Dale Manuel and Walt Pellish all seeking re-election. The position of Surveyor, which offers no salary or duties, has been vacant for a number of years.

Storm, Banks, Dougherty and Manuel faced no primary opponents and automatically advanced to the General Election. Ben Svendsen, Eva Alexander, and Josh Compton likewise faced no opposition and became the Republican challengers to Storm, Banks, and Manuel respectively. There was a contested race for the Republican nomination for Sheriff between three candidates. Additionally, Commissioner Walt Pellish drew a challenger in Caleb Hudson.

Sheriff Pete Dougherty, who had been appointed to the position in 2013, was re-elected in 2014 for the remaining two years of the term. This cycle Tom Newcomer, Tom Hansen, and Steve Sowers all filed to face Dougherty, who was eligible to serve one more four-year term.

Newcomer, whose family owned and operated The Cliffside Hotel, for many years had never sought office, but his sister, Anne Newcomer Dungan was a past chairwoman of the Jefferson County Republican Party and 2002 nominee for the West Virginia House of Delegates. He owns and operates a horse farm between Charles Town and Harpers Ferry. Both Hansen and Sowers have a background in law enforcement. Hansen retired in 2015 after 20 years with the Sheriff's Department with the position of lieutenant. Sowers, who was the Republican nominee against Dougherty in 2014, works as a law enforcement instructor.[2] The race seemed quite collegial. I recall "insiders" believing Hansen had the upper hand given his long record with the Sheriff's Department but in the end, Newcomer won the nomination with 2,210 votes to 1,474 for Hansen, and 1,017 for Sowers.

Pete Dougherty had proved to be the top local Democratic vote getter in 2014 (except for Commissioner Patsy Noland, but she ran unopposed!). This trend continued as he secured 54% of the vote to Newcomer's 46% and was returned for a final term as Sheriff.

Two other Democratic incumbents hung on against strong Republican challenges. Angie Banks and Laura Storm both ran on the efficiency of their offices, the positive customer service they offer, and the need for experience to ensure that efficiency remained. Banks faced Republican Eva Alexander, a former Democrat and substitute teacher. Storm squared off against Ben Svendsen, a stay-at-home father who had worked as a legislative aide and in county government in Northern Virginia before recently moving to Jefferson County. Both incumbents talked about their efforts to modernize the offices and ensure the public received fair, courtesy treatment. Banks was first elected in 2008 and had worked in the office prior. Storm was appointed in 2009 when the incumbent, Patsy Noland, resigned to take a seat on the County Commission, and had previously worked in the Circuit Clerk's office. Both Republicans seemed to center their campaigns around more modernization and better customer service, but neither offered specifics or instances when the incumbents hadn't done so. Banks retained her seat by two percentage points and Storm received another six-year term, tallying 53% to 47% for Svendsen.

The race for the Republican nomination for the Shepherdstown County Commission seat was not so tame as some other primaries as Walt Pellish sought a second term. His opponent, Caleb Hudson, seemed to have no campaign operation in place, with the exception of frequent social media posts, but he managed a 55% to 45% victory. While I wasn't concerning myself with the Republican Primary and I don't know all the objections the Party had to Pellish, I continually heard the refrain that he was insufficiently conservative. There was talk of him mounting a write-in campaign, but, as he was battling cancer at the time, he opted not to do so. Pellish died on February 11, 2017, shortly after his term expired.

The only Democrat to seek the Shepherdstown Commission seat was Jan C. Hafer, the Executive Director of the Shepherdstown Visitors Center. Hafer's father was a professor at Shepherd University (then College) and she grew up in Middleway and then Shepherdstown. She pursued a doctoral degree and taught for many years at Gallaudet University, before retiring and returning to Jefferson County. In an interesting turn of events, a very good friend of my mother, Scott, also taught at Gallaudet and it wasn't until 2017 that I thought to ask either if they knew one another, which they did. Hafer's contacts in Shepherdstown were extensive and she ran a visible, vigorous campaign. It came as a shock to many of us when the votes were counted in the General Election and her Republican opponent, Caleb Hudson, polled 52% of the vote. Hudson and Charles Town Commission Republican candidate Josh Compton seemed to run non-existent campaigns, with no signs, no ads, and no appearances at many local political events. Additionally, they declined to participate in several of the local debates and forums. While I've tried very hard to keep my personal feelings and partisan commentary out of this book, I will digress and say that I believe a refusal to face voters before non-partisan organizations such as the League of Women Voters and the NAACP does a disservice to the community. Be that as it may, Hafer took her loss better than I did, I think, and she continues to be active in the county, recently opening a pop-up space with her business partner in Shepherdstown.

The results from the Charles Town Commission race brought another surprise as two term Commissioner Dale Manuel was defeated by about 400 votes by Josh Compton, a social media conservative firebrand. Manuel, much like Hafer, ran a campaign that put him in front of a variety of voters across the county. A former teacher, he served many years in the WV House of Delegates, and was well known and liked. I must say I was very surprised to see him lose his seat, but in hindsight it was certainly an anti-incumbent and Republican year.

Ralph Lorenzetti was first elected as Prosecuting Attorney in 2008, after longtime incumbent Michael D. Thompson retired. No Republican had run since 1980. Two assistant prosecutors filed, Charles B. Howard and Hassan Rasheed. Howard is the son-in-law of the late Roger Ramey, who served in several leadership positions within the Democratic Party in the 1960s and 70s. Rasheed was a former officer with the Democratic Association. One Republican filed, as well, Berkeley County resident and defense attorney Matthew Harvey. State code does not require Prosecuting Attorneys to reside in the county in which they are elected, although Harvey moved to the Shepherdstown area shortly after the primary. In an active race, Rasheed tallied 56% of the vote to Howard's 44%. However, in the General he lost to Harvey, 10,228 votes to 13,096. Harvey thus became the first Republican Prosecuting Attorney in Jefferson County in at least 80 years.

The open County Clerk's seat drew a contested primary on both sides. Incumbent Jennifer Maghan was elected to the first of two terms in 2004, succeeding 36-year veteran John E. Ott. On the Republican side Joseph Maghan, the incumbent's son, and Jacki Shadle, a teacher from Middleway, vied for the nomination. Democrats chose between former County Commissioner and West Virginia State Senator Herb Snyder and minister Bill Ball, who also worked in management for AT&T. Shadle won a close race with 2,304 votes to 2,060 for Maghan while Snyder had a more comfortable victory, 3,737 votes to 2,276. The two faced off in the General and in another surprise Shadle was victorious, pulling in 12,147 votes to 11,131 for Snyder.

No candidate filed for the position of Surveyor and the position remained vacant.

Senator Herb Snyder announced his plans to retire from the Legislature at the end of his term. Patricia Rucker, who had nearly unseated Delegate Stephen Skinner of the 67th District, launched a campaign for Snyder's seat, as did Skinner. While they each ended up being their party's nominees, both had a contested primary. Skinner's announcement left the 67th District vacant. Paul Espinosa, the Delegate for the 66th District announced plans to run for Snyder's seat in the Senate but ended up not filing and instead seeking re-election to the House. 65th District Delegate Jill Upson filed for another term as well.

Let's start with the Senate seat. Snyder had first been elected to the WV Senate in 1996, was re-elected in 2000, defeated in the Primary in 2004, and then returned in 2008 and 2012. Skinner's announcement came almost right after Snyder's retirement. He had first been elected to the WV House in 2012 after Delegate John Doyle retired. Former AmeriCorps worker and SkyTruth staff member David Manthos joined the Democratic race, while former Democrat and attorney Joe Funkhouser challenged Rucker.

Manthos started off his campaign from a moderate stance, but soon veered further to the left and, I thought, was running as a more liberal alternative to Skinner. He had also served as president of the Eastern Panhandle Young Democrats and tried to capture the votes of younger voters. Skinner had a well-known name and a wide financial advantage and, unsurprisingly, won 67% to 33%.

The race on the Republican side was narrower. Rucker ran as a strongly conservative candidate and openly talked about home-schooling her children and her opposition to abortion. She surprised many with the strength of her 2014 campaign for Delegate. Funkhouser, who hailed from a well-known family in the County, had originally expressed interest in running for the 66th Delegate seat, but when Espinosa switched back to seeking re-election, Funkhouser jumped into the Senate race. An attorney with strong connections to the horseracing industry, he ran as a more business oriented conservative and I don't recall him emphasizing social issues to the degree Rucker did. In a year of insurgent conservatives, she won 55% of the vote to his 44%.

Jill Upson, who was first elected in 2014, announced her intention to run to retain her seat as the 65th District Delegate. Tiffany Lawrence, who had served from 2008 until 2014 chose not to run. David Manthos, who, as previously mentioned, was running for the Senate had flirted with seeking the seat before deciding upon the race he joined. Sammi Brown, a labor activist and political trainer, threw her hat into the ring. A graduate of Shepherd University, Brown had worked in radio before joining the labor movement. Both she and Upson faced no primary opposition, which set up the first contest between two African American female candidates for Delegate in the state. Upson was the first female African American Republican elected to the House (Delegate Minnie Buckingham Harper was the first to serve, but she was appointed to the position). While Brown had grown up in the area, she was new to local politics and ended up garnering 37% of the vote to Upson's 63%.

66th District Delegate Paul Espinosa hadn't faced a Democratic opponent in 2014, though Danny Lutz did run on the Mountain

Party line. Two Democratic Executive Committee members considering running, both Nancy Lutz and me. Lutz, who operates a farm, ended up running for Conservation District Supervisor. While I thought I could give Espinosa a run, I didn't think I could beat him, nor did I want to enter what would likely be a vitriolic campaign. Weighing heavily on my mind, too, was the death of my Mom just three months earlier, after an almost three-year battle with cancer. In the end Dave Dinges, a CSX engineer with strong labor ties, jumped into the race. An active baseball coach he and his wife, Shannon, a longtime teacher at South Jefferson Elementary, have eight children. Dinges was new to elective politics and, unfortunately, not as well known throughout the District as Espinosa. He performed ably at the debates and forums, but Espinosa skipped several, as did Upson, which made it difficult for clear distinctions between their respective positions. Espinosa ended up winning 66% of the vote to Dinges's 34%.

The race for the open 67th District brought a well-known county name and a well-known state name together. Riley Moore, the nephew of United States Senator Shelley Moore Capito and grandson of former Governor Arch Moore, jumped into the race after having recently moved to Jefferson County. He faced Daniel Scott Swisher in the Republican Primary, though Swisher didn't seem to put forth much of a campaign. He ended up winning 22% of the vote in the Primary. Democrats nominated Rod Snyder, the son of West Virginia State Senator Herb Snyder, and a former President of the Young Democrats of America. Snyder had previously sought the seat (though it was larger and numbered the 57th at the time) in 2004 but was defeated in the Primary by incumbent John Doyle. Moore and Snyder both raised and spent liberally. In a Republican year the usually blue 67th District changed to red with Moore winning 4,230 votes to Snyder's 4,134.

When the dust settled from the Legislative races, State Senator John Unger was the only Democrat left in the delegation covering

Jefferson County. For the first time in almost a hundred years no Democrat represented Jefferson County in the WV House of Delegates.

[1] Eric Eyre "Gainer to Work for White Collar Crime Center," *Charleston Gazette* (Charleston, WV) Apr. 26, 2016.

[2] Richard Belisle "Three Vie for GOP Nod in Jefferson County Sheriff Race," *Herald-Mail* (Hagerstown, MD) Nov. 4, 2016.

14

The Election of 2018

If 2016 was a revolt against local Democratic candidates, 2018 was a shift back to a sort of 50/50 balance of power. I'd be naïve if I didn't acknowledge the role the Rockwool industrial plant played in some of the Democratic victories, but I think Democratic voters who previously stayed on the sidelines were newly energized by the behavior, and perhaps the policies, of President Donald Trump.

As an off-year election, there wasn't nearly the long list of offices on the ballot as in 2016. Voters had the opportunity to elect a United States Senator, a member of the United States House, a State Senator, three State Delegates, two County Commissioners, three Board of Education members, a Conservation District Supervisor, and two Supreme Court Justices.

Incumbent United States Senator, and the only Democrat in the state's Congressional delegation, Joe Manchin, III decided to seek a second, full term. He faced Paula Jean Swearengin in the Democratic Primary. As I've stated before, I am not always on the same page as Senator Manchin when it comes to the issues, but I do realize that electing a moderate to conservative Democrat in West Virginia is often the best we will achieve as a Party. As much as I adore Maria Cantwell from Washington or Mazie Hirono of Hawaii, a majority of West Virginia voters just aren't on the same policy page as those Senators, but they are with Manchin.

Swearengin styled herself as a populist progressive and been a vocal support of Bernie Sanders in 2016. Her activism in West Virginia has been heavily environmentally focused, especially focused on ending mountain top removal mining. She ran to the left of Manchin on most issues and was supported by the Justice Democrats and Brand New Congress. She did not have the retail political skill of Manchin, though. While many of the progressive Democrats throughout the state supported her, she ended up capturing only 30% of the vote to Manchin's 70%.

The Republican Primary for the US Senate was much larger and featured some familiar names. Those vying to take on Manchin included WV Attorney General Patrick Morrisey, US Representative Evan Jenkins, felon and coal magnate Don Blankenship, veteran Tom Willis, and two more. Morrisey had a base of support in the Eastern Panhandle and with many newer, Republican residents of the state. Jenkins, I believed, was the establishment favorite and considered to be the most electable of the candidates, given his ability to defeat Democratic incumbents, both in Primaries (when he was a Democrat) and General Elections. Blankenship was WV's own version of Donald Trump and, at one point, seemed to be the odds-on favorite. His bombastic statements and legal problems, hopefully, torpedoed his chances. Willis didn't get a lot of attention, but he was also an Eastern Panhandle resident and seemed to be in the, once popular, Liz Cheney, John McCain lane of Republican politics, that of hawkish foreign policy and conservative economic and domestic policies.

President Trump went so far as to encourage WV Republicans to vote for either Morrisey or Jenkins, and not Blankenship, out of fear that he would hand Manchin an easy re-election race. Morrisey scooted by Jenkins with 35% to 29% with Blankenship at 20% and Willis at 10%. West Virginia was certainly considered a prime pick-up for Republicans given the sharp rightward tilt in recent years.

I did find that most of the left-leaning Democrats who had supported Swearengin "came home" to Manchin by the General. The Senator won re-election by a very close 50% to 46% with 4% going to Libertarian Rusty Hollen. Interestingly, Morrisey lost in his home county, Jefferson, a first for him. Even though incumbent Democratic Senators lost in other red states, including North Dakota, Missouri, and Indiana, Manchin was able to hold on in one of the most pro-Trump states in the country.

Incumbent US Representative Alex Mooney sought re-election and two Democrats vied for the opportunity to challenge him. Combat veteran and director for The Mission Continues Aaron Scheinberg and former Hillary Clinton advisor Talley Sergent each argued they were the stronger candidate. Scheinberg and his family had recently moved back to Berkeley County, where his grandparents had lived, a strikingly similar dynamic to many families in the Eastern Panhandle. Sergent was from the other end of the district, Kanawha County, and had worked for Senator Rockefeller and Coca-Cola, in addition to her position with Clinton.

I supported Scheinberg throughout the Primary, as I believed his profile was one which fit the district very well, in addition to his geographic position. Both candidates had a strong history of and desire to continue public service, but it seemed to me a military veteran from the Eastern Panhandle had a shot at defeating Mooney. I was also troubled by the rhetoric of some of Sergent's supporters indicating that Scheinberg wasn't a real West Virginian, as he hadn't been born and hadn't lived fulltime in West Virginia for his entire life. Given the fact that our state continues to bleed population, especially younger people,

I found that language to be both xenophobic and self-defeatist. Again, I want to stress that I don't think this was due to Sergent, herself, but rather overzealous campaign surrogates and supporters. Issue by issue there wasn't a lot of difference between the candidates, though. In the end Sergent received 63% to Scheinberg's 37%.

After the Primary, Scheinberg committed to help Sergent and campaign with her. She focused very heavily on Mooney's absenteeism throughout the District and his general lack of support for the needs of West Virginians. A third candidate appeared on the ballot, too, Jefferson County's Danny Lutz, who ran as a Mountain Party candidate. Sergent received the backing of Emily's List and ran a very energetic campaign, however she came up short, receiving 43% of the vote to Mooney's 54%, with Lutz taking 3%. It should be noted that Sergent performed the best of the three Democrats running for the US House in West Virginia and improved over Mark Hunt's performance in 2016.

All state legislative officials in Jefferson County indicated they planned to run again, Senator John Unger, Delegates Jill Upson (65th), Paul Espinosa (66th), and Riley Moore (67th). Unger, of course, was the only Democrat representing Jefferson County in Charleston, but that was set to change. Unger faced off against Delegate Mike Folk (63rd) who had made headlines in 2016 by tweeting Hillary Clinton should be "hung [sic] on the Mall in Washington, DC."[1]

A commercial airline pilot for United Airlines, he was suspended from flight over those comments for a period as well. Delegates Upson and Espinosa faced familiar Democratic challengers as 2016 nominees Sammi Brown and Dave Dinges were again nominated by voters. Moore drew an interesting challenger, former WV Delegate John Doyle, who had served in the House for one term in the 80s and then again from 1992 until 2012, when he retired to take a position with the State Department of Revenue.

Interestingly both Espinosa and Moore faced primary opponents. Middleway resident and real estate agent Reese Clabaugh challenged Espinosa. He had previously run against Jane Tabb in the 2012 Republican Primary for County Commission. Moore's 2016 opponent Dan Swisher returned for a second run. Espinosa led with 63% to 37% for Clabaugh, while Moore polled 80% of the vote compared to Swisher's 20%. The word on the street indicated that both Clabaugh and Swisher ran to the right of the incumbents.

Unger's role as a minister with several area churches and his community involvement, without a doubt, aided in him retaining his seat. Additionally, as one of the more moderate members of the WV Senate, he did have crossover appeal with conservative Independents and Republican voters. When all votes were cast, Unger was elected to a sixth term, with approximately 52% of the vote, owing to his strength in the Jefferson County portion of the district. He improved upon his 2014 showing when he faced former Delegate Larry Faircloth.

Democratic victories continued as Delegates Upson and Moore were defeated by 47% to 53% and 44% to 56% respectively. Dinges improved upon his 2016 performance, receiving 42% of the vote, but Espinosa prevailed. There are collectively five legislative seats that cover Jefferson County (two State Senate seats and three State House seats). Prior to 2018, Republicans held a 4-1 advantage. When the dust settled after 2018, the number stood at 3-2 in favor of Democrats. The Party also made modest gains across the state in House races.

The race between Sammi Brown and Jill Upson was definitely a contrast to 2016 when both candidates seemed to rely upon support with their bases to push them on to victory. Upson was slow to start her campaign, perhaps operating under the assumption that her strong showing from two years prior would continue. Brown hit the ground running and never seemed to stop knocking on doors and meeting with voters. In a fairly divided district, Upson ran as a conversative and Brown as a pragmatic progressive. Brown, also, was vocal in her opposition to the Rockwool plant, something Upson dodged quite frequently.

No longer a first-time candidate, Dinges utilized some of the experience gained from his previous race to hammer Espinosa on his support for Rockwool, which is housed in the 66th District and in close proximity to North Jefferson Elementary, TA Lowery Elementary, and the Fox Glen development. Dinges's union ties were in full effect, too, as he garnered support from the teachers' unions and other labor groups. I think, however, Espinosa's history with the long-term residents of the District enabled a sort of going with "the devil you know" syndrome to occur. He certainly had to work that cycle, though, to maintain his seat.

I have to admit I was quite excited to have John Doyle file to run for his old seat. Doyle was in office when I first became involved in Democratic politics, and I can always remember my parents speaking of him. Given his long record of service to the community, he was an ideal candidate to take on Moore. Recently retired, as well, he had the opportunity and energy to campaign full time and make the effort his prime focus. It seems to me that Moore believed he could spend six figures and win without a problem. Clearly, he was mistaken.

An extra County Commission seat was unexpectedly open owing to the resignation of Harpers Ferry Commissioner Eric Bell on June 21st, 2016. Bell, who had been elected in 2014, was accused of possessing child pornography, sexual abuse of a minor by a person of trust, and other charges.[2] He was elected in an upset in 2014 against Democrat Ronda Lehman. In the case of a vacancy on the Commission, applications are sought, and the rest of the body appoints a replacement, of the same party as the one who resigned, to serve until the next regular election. The four remaining County Commissioners appointed Peter Onoszko to the vacancy, as he had been the runner up in the 2014 Republican Primary. Eighteen applications were received, including one from former Democratic Charles Town Commissioner Greg Lance, 2018 Republican candidate Gary Cogle, and 2018 Mountain Party candidate David Tabb.

There was a three-way race for both party nominations. Democrats picked between former County Prosecuting Attorney Ralph Lorenzetti, Lance (who was again a Democrat), and Harpers Ferry Town Recorder Kevin Carden. Republican options were Onoszko, Cogle, and Tabb. There wasn't much space between the Democrats, with all voicing at least moderate opposition to Rockwool. All three had prior experience in elective office and the contest remained quite civil. On the Republican side Tabb made his opposition to Rockwool a key element of his campaign. Cogle benefited from strong support among the Republican leaning farming community, while Onoszko seemed to enjoy a boost from the Republican Party leadership. On Election Day Onoszko tallied 1,548 votes to Cogle's 1,391 and Tabb's 794, while Lorenzetti won the Democratic Primary with 1,896 votes, followed by Lance with 1,039, and Carden at 975.

Tabb switched his party registration from Republican to Mountain and jumped into the General Election after having been chosen at their nominating convention, thus setting up the first three-way candidate race for County Commission since 2010. Much of the campaign oxygen was consumed by Rockwool, with Lorenzetti and Tabb opposing its continued construction. Another issue of note was the proposed removal of a plaque on the front wall of the Jefferson County Court House which honored Confederate soldiers from the County. The County Commission voted 3-2 to have it remain with Onoszko, Josh Compton, and Caleb Hudson supporting the decision to have to remain in place. Commissioners Patsy Noland and Jane Tabb opposed the decision. Lorenzetti repeatedly stated he would vote to remove the plaque, thus providing a majority if Tabb was re-elected. (Had she not, her Democrat opponent supported removing it, too). Lorenzetti also made a point throughout the campaign for the need to return civility to all levels of politics, but specifically, within his ability, to the county level. I think this resonated with many voters at the county level, just as it did across the country when offered as a campaign plank. On Election Night 2018, Lorenzetti received 51% of the vote to 42% for Onoszko, and 7% for Tabb, making him the third occupant of the seat in less than three years. Lorenzetti was sworn in almost right away, as his victory was for the remainder of Bell's term, which also meant he had to run again in 2020.

The only Commission seat that was scheduled to be up in 2018 was the Middleway seat, occupied by Jane Tabb from 2001-2007 and again since 2013. As earlier stated, she had faced opposition in the 2012 Republican Primary from Reece Clabaugh, winning by 370 votes. 2018 would prove to be much tougher. While it's sometimes hard to apply a liberal/moderate/conservative label to County Commission decisions and votes, the term "moderate" has often been applied to Tabb as she has differed from positions taken by other Republicans on the Commission from time to time. The most recent examples include her vocal opposition to Rockwool during the campaign and her support to remove the Confederate plaque, as well as support for the ambulance fee program. As I am chairman of the Democratic Party, I don't often hear much about the inner workings of the Republican Party in Jefferson County and am, often, confused as to why Tabb hasn't enjoyed more support from her own party.

This time around Jack Hefestay, a retired Navy captain and member of the Republican Executive Committee, challenged Tabb from her right.[3] There was much talk in the County of Democrats who knew Tabb deciding to support her by changing their party registration to Independent so they could vote for her in the Primary Election. The only Democrat on the Commission at the time, Patsy Noland, went so far as to endorse Tabb for re-election and publicly announce her intention to re-register as an Independent simply to support Tabb. In the end the effort worked as Tabb squeaked past Hefestay by 40 votes out of 3,882 cast. Since that time Hefestay has become the chairman of the Republican Executive Committee but has since stepped down.

To digress for a moment, some of the Democrats who registered as Independents to support Tabb were also very vocal in their support of specific Democratic candidates and were, thus, unable to vote for any Democrat in that Primary, including those in contested primaries. While the numbers aren't likely to have shifted sufficient support to have changed the outcomes, I remain puzzled why Democrats left their own party and candidates behind to support one Republican candidate.

The Democratic race for the Middleway seat was somewhat muddled from the start. Former Commissioner Frances Morgan, who had beaten Tabb in 2006, but was then defeated by Tabb in 2012 chose not to run, as did a number of other District residents. I would be dishonest to not acknowledge that I flirted with the possibility of running and had received a surprising number of supportive comments, but my Dad had suffered a stroke about four months prior and I didn't feel as though I could campaign effectively. On the final day of filing Carol Grant decided to run and was unopposed. I'd known Carol for a number of years, and she was very active in many civic organizations, including the Democratic Party. Her professional background was in accounting and strategic planning, and she had retired as the top civilian at the US Coast Guard. Oddly, though, Grant withdrew after the Primary was over and one of my first acts as the new chairman of the Democratic Executive Committee was to lead the process of finding a candidate. Sadly, Carol passed away after a very quick bout with cancer on January 11th of 2019.

Answering the advertisement for the vacant ballot line was Robert Barrat of Shenandoah Junction. This was my first-time meeting Robert, though I recall both of my parents speaking of him over the years as a good Democrat. Barrat, a Jefferson County native, was engaged in farming and then joined the Air National Guard in Martinsburg. After graduating from law school, he began to practice in the Panhandle, while maintaining his farm, which, unfortunately, backs up to Rockwool's property. I didn't envy the short amount of time he had to introduce himself to voters, but he certainly worked very hard and more than earned every vote he received.

As the campaign unfolded, there wasn't a lot of room between the candidates on the issues. Both talked about their concern involving Rockwool, with Barrat perhaps being a bit more assertive on the need for the project to be stopped, the need for emergency services to be supported, and the removal of the Confederate plaque. Once the votes were counted Tabb was returned for another term, winning 10,832 votes to Barrat's 9,666, with an oddly high 121 (or over half a percent) write-in votes.

Tabb's victory meant a majority of the County Commissioners were still registered Republicans, though from perhaps different wings of the Party. It also meant Commissioner Noland didn't become the lone woman on the Commission. Shortly after Lorenzetti's swearing in, a vote was taken to remove the Confederate plaque which passed 3-2 (Commissioners Compton and Hudson voted no).

Two Circuit Court seats were open after only two years since they were last filed. Judge John Yoder died in June from complications relating to cardiac surgery.[4] Judge Gray Silver, III, resigned his seat citing health concerns in December of 2017.[5] The Governor is empowered to appoint a replacement for a Circuit Judge and the appointee then runs in the next election. Governor Jim Justice appointed Morgan County Prosecuting Attorney Debra McLaughlin to Judge Yoder's seat and attorney Steven Redding to Judge Silver's seat. With McLaughlin's appointment, half of the circuit judges were women for the first time in history. Redding had been an unsuccessful candidate for the seat now held by Judge Bridget Cohee in 2016. Redding had already been running for Silver's vacant seat at the time of his appointment.

Both seats saw contested races. Martinsburg attorney David Hammer filed to run against McLaughlin. Family Court Judge David Camilletti (who had lost to Silver in 2000 by 39 votes) and former Assistant Prosecuting Attorney Kim Crockett, joined Redding in running for Silver's seat. After spirited campaigns Hammer unseated McLaughlin (who would later be appointed to another vacant seat), and Redding retained his seat.

Regularly scheduled for the Primary Election were three Board of Education seats, those held by Scott Sudduth, Laurie Ogden, and Kathy Skinner. All three filed for re-election along with Jefferson County Schools Cultural Diversity Facilitator and Staff Development Coordinator Arthena Roper, teacher Donna Joy, retired teacher and staffer for former Congressman Harley O. Staggers, Jr. Jim Watkins, author and retired businessman Tom Poteet, and preschool teacher and recent Washington High School graduate Aaron Hackett. In a surprising move, the Jefferson County Education Association declined to endorse any of the incumbents and instead chose Roper, Watkins, and Poteet. Once the ballots were counted Ogden and Skinner retained their seats and Roper came in third, bumping Sudduth off the Board by almost 400 votes.

With the election of Roper and re-election of Ogden and Skinner, the Board now had its first African American woman ever and was majority female again for the first time since 2007.

The race for Conservation District Supervisor was a repeat of 2016 with Nancy Lutz and Richard F. Blue both filing. Lutz was elected to the remaining two years of the term in 2016 and she edged out Blue again 3,729 to 3,583.

Originally, I wasn't going to write too much about the turmoil experienced by the West Virginia Supreme Court throughout 2018, but I decided to offer up what I remember of the various actions taken against the Court. Sitting at that time were Justices Allen Loughry, Margaret Workman, Robin Jean Davis, Menis Ketchum, and Beth Walker. On August 13th, the West Virginia House of Delegates impeached all five Supreme Court Justices, the first time in American history that ever happened.

Owing to reports of overspending by the Court, the United States Attorney for the Southern District of West Virginia opened an investigation which resulted in an official audit of the body's finances. A myriad of concerns was found, including expensive renovations to offices, use of state vehicles outside of the accepted parameters, and improper reporting of wages for Senior Status Judges. Justice Loughry was also found to have removed a Cass Gilbert desk from the Capitol and had it transported to his home for personal use. He had also been removed as Chief Justice by the other Justices earlier in 2018 for lying and failing to disclose, to them, he had been served with a federal subpoena in 2017. Additionally, Justices Loughry and Ketchum utilized state vehicles without reporting the usage on their tax returns.[6]

On June 26th, the House of Delegates met in special session to consider impeachment proceedings. On July 11th, Justice Ketchum resigned from the Court and three weeks later he pleaded guilty to one count of wire fraud. Around a month later the House Judiciary Committee recommended the four remaining Justices be impeached. In the case of Justice Loughry the recommendation was made owing to his lack of oversight, improper removal of the previously mentioned desk, improper use of a government computer, improper use of state-owned cars, overspending on office renovations, overpaying Senior

Status Judges, and lying to the Legislature. Justices Workman and Davis were accused of overpaying Senior Status Judges, permitting a lack of oversight, and overspending on renovations. Justice Walker's recommended impeachment revolved around a lack of oversight and overspending. On August 13th, the House impeached the four remaining Justices. The next day Justice Davis tendered her resignation to be retroactively effective the day prior.[7]

On August 20th, the West Virginia Senate met to organize for the trials. The pretrial hearings began on September 11th and the Senate voted 15-19 to try Justice Davis even though she had resigned from the Court.

On October 1st, Justice Walker's trial began and concluded the next day. A vote of 31-1-1 to not remove her from office passed. Senator Weld was absent, and Senator Baldwin was the lone vote to convict. She was reprimanded publicly and censured.[8]

Justice Workman's trial began was set to begin two weeks later, but a temporary Supreme Court, populated by five Circuit Judges, blocked the trial ruling that the articles of impeachment violated the separation of powers doctrine and that they lacked standing to proceed. Her trial was to begin on October 15th and on that day the Senate was gaveled into session and then adjourned without action against Workman.

Justice Davis's trial was to begin on October 29th, but the Court's ruling that Workman couldn't be tried also applied to Davis. No further action was taken against her.

The last pending trial was that of Justice Loughry and was to begin on November 12th. Again, the ruling of the Court applying to Justice Workman also applied to him. However, a federal criminal trial had already concluded on October 12[th,] and he was convicted of seven counts of wire fraud, one count of mail fraud, one count of witness tampering, and two counts of lying to the FBI. He resigned from the Court on November 12th.[9] He was sentenced to 2 years in federal prison on February 13th, 2019, and was sent to Salters, South Carolina to the Federal Correctional Institution, Williamsburg. On December 19th, 2020, he was released.[10]

So, the Court clearly went through a lot in a fairly short amount of time. Governor Justice had two appointments to make in 2018, those to take the seats of Justices Ketchum and Davis. Tim Armstead, the West Virginia Speaker of the House, was appointed to Justice Ketchum's seat on August 25th, 2018. He then ran in the Special Election for the seat which was for a term to run through January 1st, 2021. Justice Davis's seat went to Congressman Evan Jenkins, right after he lost the Primary for United States Senate. He won the Special Election and received a six-year term on the Court.

I want to discuss the Special Elections for a moment. Thanks to the appointments by Governor Justice, both Justice Jenkins and Justice Armstead were able to run as incumbents and said they would each return trust and dignity to the court. Each of the contests saw 10 candidates file. Given the quantity of candidates and the extremely short campaign, many voters were overwhelmed with choices.

The candidates seeking the Division 1 seat were: Armstead; Williamson attorney Robert Carlton; D.C. Offutt, an attorney in Barboursville; Harry Bruner, Jr., a Charleston attorney; Huntington attorney Ronald Hatfield, Jr.; former WV Delegate and 2016 Second Congressional District nominee Mark Hunt of Charleston; Hiram "Bucky" Lewis, a frequent candidate for statewide office; Kanawha County Circuit Judge Joanna Tabit; Circuit Judge Chris Wilkes from Martinsburg; and Jeff Wood, an attorney from Nitro.[11]

Division 2 saw the following candidates: Jenkins; Family Court Judge Jim Douglas from Kanawha County; Lewisburg attorney Robert Frank; former WV Senate President and 2011 and 2016 candidate for Governor Jeff Kessler of Glen Dale; Brenden Long, an attorney from Hurricane; Wheeling attorney Jim O'Brien; William Schwartz, an attorney from Charleston; Dennise Smith, also an attorney from Charleston; Marty Sheehan, a Wheeling based attorney; and Boone County Circuit Judge William Thompson.[12]

The top vote getters in Division 1 were Armstead at 26%, Tabit at 22%, Wilkes at 13%, and Hunt with 12%. Division 2 saw Jenkins re-elected with 36%, Smith at 14%, Kessler with 12%, and Douglas at 9%. Wilkes, with his base in the Eastern Panhandle won Jefferson County with Tabit second. Smith came in first in Jefferson for Division 2.

I supported Tabit and Smith and was disappointed to both come in second rather than first. They were, also, the only women out of 20 total candidates, which is a bit surprising. Had they both been elected the Court would have had a record four female members. Clearly there was a desire to among a majority of voters to see Justices other than Armstead and Jenkins on the Court, as they both won with pluralities.

The backdrop of the trouble with the West Virginia Supreme Court definitely put a damper on what was otherwise a strong year for the Democratic Party in West Virginia. I am still surprised they were unable to capture at least one of the Supreme Court seats. (Of course, they are non-partisan, but both Armstead and Jenkins were elected to previous offices as Republicans.) Only United States House of Representatives candidate Talley Sergent, Dave Dinges, and Robert Barrat came up short, though all three improved upon the performance of the last Democrat to seek that office.

[1] Doni Bloomfield, "United Airlines Suspends Pilot-Lawmaker Who Called for Hanging Hillary Clinton," *Chicago Tribune* (Chicago, IL) Jul. 18, 2016.

[2] Richard Belisle, "Jefferson County Commissioner Resigns Amid Sex Abuse Charges," *Herald Mail* (Hagerstown, MD) Jun. 21, 2016.

[3] "Hefestay Challenges Tabb for Jefferson County Commission Seat," *Herald Mail* (Hagerstown, MD), Apr. 24, 2018.

[4] Matthew Umstead, "Eastern Panhandle Judge Dies from Complications After Heart Surgery," *Herald-Mail* (Hagerstown, MD) Jun. 9, 2017.

[5] Matthew Umstead, "Eastern Panhandle Judge Cites Health, Family Reasons for Retirement," *Herald-Mail* (Hagerstown, MD) Dec. 12, 2017.

[6] Brad McElhinny, "Justice Loughry Named in 32-Count Judicial Complaint Saying He Lived Over and Over," *MetroNews* (Charleston, WV), Jun. 6, 2018.

[7] Brad McElhinny, "Delegates Vote to Impeach All Four Remaining WV Supreme Court Justices," *MetroNews* (Charleston, WV), Aug. 7, 2018.

[8] "Senators Reprimand Justice Walker, But Vote to Not Impeach," *WSAZ* (Huntington, WV), Sep. 27, 2018.

[9] Kennie Bass and Jeff Morris, "West Virginia Supreme Court Justice Loughry Convicted on 11 Charges," *WCHS* (Charleston, WV), Oct. 12, 2018.

[10] Phil Kabler, "Former Supreme Court Justice Loughry Sentenced to 24 Months in Federal Prison," *Charleston Gazette-Mail* (Charleston, WV), Feb. 13, 2019.

[11] Steven Allen Adams, "Justice Appoints Armstead, Jenkins to Supreme Court," *Weirton Daily Times* (Weirton, WV), Aug. 26, 2018.

[12] Ibid.

15

Looking Ahead

2020 turned out to be something of a redo of 2016. Democratic candidates who were thought to have the inside track ended up losing and West Virginia became even more of a Republican state. I think many of us are still digesting the results from this year's election, so I won't go into detail about what happened. Perhaps I can save that for another volume of this book sometime in the future.

I've strived to ensure this is a book that doesn't extol the virtues of only one political party or movement, and further have tried to ensure I'm not making it a political manifesto or taking an unfair stand for only one movement or idea. However, I do want to offer a brief paragraph or two relating to how I see things moving forward in Jefferson County and West Virginia.

While Jefferson County remains one of the counties most open to both political parties, as is evidenced by having both a Democrat and a Republican serving the same district in the State Senate, and both Democrats and Republicans being viable candidates for countywide offices, I fear we are losing something that was still in place when I first became involved in politics. There was a time when Democratic and Republican candidates could meet in a friendly atmosphere and discuss the issues facing our community. I feel as though that time has come to an end. Hopefully, though, it is only temporary.

There has never been any doubt in my mind about being a Democrat. I felt no pressure from my parents in the formation of my political beliefs. I went to a Catholic high school where I was one of the few liberal students in my class of 48. (Though, of course, as teenagers I doubt many of us had formed our full, adult policy ideas.) Even though I've always believed in the idea that government is a system to assist, not oppress, I felt no need to distance myself or denigrate Republicans. I'm proud to consider some of our former Republican officeholders to be friends and people to whom I've looked up. We could identify the areas in which we agreed, discuss those issues on which we disagreed, and leave friends. Conservative candidates like Fred Blackmer and Gary Dungan have been some of the friendliest people I remember meeting in Jefferson County politics. County Commissioners like Al Hooper and Greg Corliss, whether they realized it or not, offered mentorship to me in how I viewed the politics of Jefferson County. As I write this, I'm not sure I recognize local politics anymore.

We seem to have moved entirely into two camps, not necessarily bound by political affiliation. The outrageously vocal, vitriolic, and venomous online presence of organizations like Jefferson Prosperity and their followers has truly poisoned our community. Not only has it made politics less attractive to many local residents, but it has also caused a deep depression in the number of candidates opting to run for office. I can only hope we will move beyond this as the years pass.

Our county and state are facing great challenges and we need elected officials, from both parties, who are well informed on the issues and willing to sit down and work together. I sincerely hope we can see this happen in the not-too-distant future.

Howard Stafford Leigh Koonce is a life-long resident of Jefferson County and can trace his family roots in the area back to the late 18th century. He was educated at Saint Maria Goretti High School, the Presidential Classroom, and Shepherd University. Professionally he was worked as a freelance journalist, bookseller, private tutor, non-profit organizer, and political organizer. His short fiction has appeared in *The Charleston Anvil*, *Sans Merci*, and *Mind Murals*, while his journalism has been featured in *West Virginia Graffiti*, *The Observer*, *The Spirit of Jefferson*, and *The Shepherdstown Chronicle*. He spent time on Capitol Hill as a Congressional Intern for Senator Jay Rockefeller, and late worked for a PAC in DC. Leigh is obsessed with political history, *Scooby-Doo* cartoons, *Archie* comics, the Shetland Islands, and the cats and dogs of Shepherdstown and the surrounding areas.